PROPHETIC REFORMATION

INCLUDING

The Prophetic Story of Mankind

Stephen G. Duame

Gleaners Field Press

Hallandale Beach, Florida

PROPHETIC REFORMATION – First Edition (1.15)

ISBN: 978-0-9960821-2-9

PropheticReformation.org

DEDICATION

One evening, several days before Easter (Resurrection Sunday), my parents took our family to hear a guest speaker somewhere in the Turtle Mountains of North Dakota. 'We'll have an Easter service if Jesus hasn't returned,' the speaker noted repeatedly. Even as an eight-year-old little boy, his words somehow made sense to me.

But, later that night, I couldn't sleep. I wasn't sure I was ready for Jesus' return. I crept downstairs to my parent's room and knocked on the door. 'I'm a sinner,' I said sobbing. They knew what I was trying to say. My father, a Lutheran pastor of four country churches at the time, took me to the dining room table and led me in a sinner's prayer of salvation. Looking back, that experience clearly changed the direction of my life.

For me and countless others, my parents have been faithful servants of the Lord. Always laying down their own lives for the benefit of others. They cultivated numerous different 'outreaches', while struggling with the care of their own large family. Their passionate faithfulness in word and deed is the background of my life.

My father's love of the Scriptures, both Old and New Testaments, the ministry of the church, and his love of Israel and the Jewish people, positively biased my perspective on reality. My parents taught me from an early age what was important in life. My father's teachings, especially on prophecy, afforded me a great head start in my own search to understand 'end-times'.

That special evening instilled in me a lifelong passion to understand Biblical prophecy, and the desire to somehow participate in the return of Jesus. Not fully understanding what that meant in those days I would later describe it in very practical terms. To friends, I would simply say my desire was, "to prepare the way of the Lord, even if that meant building bleachers on the Mt. of Olives." Thank you, mom and dad, (Earle and Arlene Duame).

ACKNOWLEDGEMENT

What do we have that we did not receive? (1 Corinthians 4:7) There have been so many important people who have added to my life's journey.

But today, I want to acknowledge and thank my two good friends and partners who have made the last few years more effective and enjoyable – Larry Hawkes and Michael Brauner. Through many, many, hours of discussion and study, abstract ideas have been verbalized and formalized. Thank you for your faithfulness, friendship, and many talents. And thanks, Larry, for financial and editing assistance at critical times.

Also, to my good friend Dr. Jeff Hazim (and company), whose dynamic study group, years ago, was for me a kind of prophetic 'coming-out party.' In them I found both challenging and competent partners, in whom we were all able to sharpen each other's gifts for the Lord's service. Jeff was also the first to attempt to capture some of the elements of this new Genesis 41 prophetic vision by writing his wonderful book "The Heart of David" (and a major editor of this book).

Continuing recently, we have started a new study group that has materialized into a group called Prophetic Reformation Ministry. Some of that material was used to create "Section One: PROPHETIC REFORMATION" and contributed to renaming this book.

And also, to my brother John Duame, who early on was one of the first to accept these prophetic views, and more recently gave important financial support during the preliminary formation of this book, at great discomfort. Thanks John.

TABLE OF CONTENTS

First

This book describes a new prophetic story. Ironically, there is nothing new about that. However, if you persevere you will find a uniquely serious and challenging model of end-of-the-age Biblical prophecy. To help our readers quickly get a sense of what this prophecy model is about, many of the fundamental concepts and Scriptures foundational to our model are summarized in lists found in Appendix B: The End-of-the-Age by the Numbers.

But before you think of going there, Appendix A: A Personal-Discovery Exercise has an exercise you might want to try. We believe the end-of-the-age is centered on unique key elements found in Jesus' prophetic sermon in Mathew 24. By taking the Personal-Discovery Exercise before you read the book, you may discover the key elements for yourself. However, whether you do the exercise or not, we highly stress the point that at a minimum, you should read the 'Short Answer' found in Appendix A at the end of this book.

My Personal Journey

An early part of my personal story is found in the Dedication above. Continuing in that life journey, prophecy was a passionate and consistent driving force. Beyond the typical study and searching through available sources, from time to time, major breakthroughs were experienced. To inject a greater sense of a real process, I will relate just several of those as an important background for the now much greater, systematic story told here in this book.

In the 1980's I discovered the Feasts of the Lord and how God uses them as a backdrop to virtually everything he does. He uses these 'appointed times' to form his 'calendar of events'. I began to adjust my life to their rhythm, such as observing the Feasts as Sabbaths, which often gave me time for extra spiritual study and contemplation.

I came to understand that Yom Teruah, the Feast of Trumpets, usually referred to as Rosh Hashanah, was the Jewish New Year. I further learned of Judaism's weekly Torah readings, the Parashot, or portions. The Sages have taken the first five books of the Old Testament (Torah) and divided them into 54 weekly portions which are read, one each Sabbath, throughout the year. They begin a new Torah reading cycle each New Year.

Deciding to do likewise, in 1993 I also began a new 'read through the Bible' cycle on Rosh Hashanah. By the Feast of Tabernacles (a seven-day Feast, fifteen days later), I had reached Genesis 41.

As I read the account of Pharaoh's dream and Joseph, I was overwhelmed by the nature of these patterns. Years of prophecy study had prepared me with lots and lots of prophetic 'pieces' and several tentative overall frameworks, though none, for me, were set in stone.

The typical seven-year Revelation models just couldn't systematically accommodate many prophetic passages and ideas. As my mind ticked through those ideas like a mental rolodex, I began to pace back and forth in excitement. Using Pharaoh's dream as a pattern, "What if there was a seven-year period BEFORE the Revelation story?" "Yes, Yes, Yes, that would work!" I kept thinking to myself. Almost immediately I felt I had hit prophetic gold. I remember getting into a friend's SUV that week going to a "Concerts of Prayer". "I think I have discovered the key to all prophecy", I told him.

I was confident then, and I am many times more confident of that statement today after 25+ years of study, especially with today's access to the Internet, etc. With the Genesis 41 framework, prophecy becomes beautiful.

There is a certain special 'beauty' to the fact that the 'key' to the 'end' is found in the 'beginning' (of the Bible). Isn't that just like God? From a God who claims to know the end at the beginning, one would expect the beginning to reveal the end. And so, it does.

Beauty! Here are two such examples:

Genesis 41 is the start of Judaism's tenth weekly Torah reading (the number 10 represents 'completion' in Biblical numerology); its name is, "At the end"; how appropriate.

And second, the second dream of Pharaoh was described like this:

He fell asleep again and had a second dream: <u>Seven heads of grain, healthy and good, were growing on a single stalk</u>. (Genesis 41:5)

Do you see it? What is the word picture underlined above? It is clearly a menorah, Judaism's symbol of light and revelation (also used many times in the Book of Revelation). God uses a hidden symbol of light to reveal the hidden key to all prophecy. Again, how beautiful!

Remarkably, the dream that would become the key to all prophecy was given to the 'world' (Pharaoh) first. But the interpretation and execution of that prophecy fell to Joseph.

For me, hidden in Pharaoh's dreams, and all subsequent findings derived from them, is the prophetic framework in which all end-of-the-age prophetic events find their context. Without this essential context, prophetic events are subject to the 'cut and paste', arbitrary speculations of eager expositors—never to be fully understood or completed.

Line upon line, precept upon precept; truth begets truth (error dead-ends)! Like a series of dominos, one by one, week after week, each succeeding truth fell into place. As I extended the search backwards, toward that critical 'first spark' event of the end-of-the-age over the next several years, the shocking reality of the 'kingdom exodus' and the 'journey', fell into place.

With that, the essential framework seems to be complete. We now have the prophetically significant and often utilized framework of a 'three day's journey' (from Egypt into the Promised Land) framing the end-of-the-age. Again, how beautiful! The institution of Israel began with a 'three-days-journey' and so also, will the 'kingdom' on earth.

Years later I would discover Jesus would point back to this story of Joseph as the second commission in his Matthew 24 survey (v. 45). Further study of Mathew 24 discovered that Jesus' survey identifies the Exodus, 'this generation' born in the wilderness, and the conquest of the Promised Land, as HIS end-of the-age framework as well, the model we describe in this book.

There are likely more surprises and flesh to add to this superstructure, but collectively, this Journey story appears to beautifully explain how the kingdom comes to earth. It gives us the context for the final 'testimony given to all nations' before 'the end' can come.

In the early stages, I was often asked who the book was written for. Over time I realized the best answer was, "For me". As any author knows, the discipline of translating complex and sometimes incomplete thoughts into communicable ideas is extremely beneficial. It certainly has been for me. In a very real sense this book is just a continuation of my personal journey.

However, I now have some exceptional friends who have joined me in this journey. They feel it is time to give it to a wider audience, and I agree. Once we hear your response, any deficiencies this book can be remedied in future releases, perhaps some even written by you.

I am truly grateful for the past and excited for what lays before us.

We welcome your comments. To comment or see the comments of others, and for more information see:

PropheticReformation.org or comments@PropheticReformation.org
Stephen

Section One
PROPHETIC
REFORMATION

"I have much more to say to you, more than you can now bear. But when he, the Spirit of truth, comes, he will guide you into all truth. ... and he will tell you what is yet to come. (John 16: 12-13)

A STATEMENT ON PROPHETIC REFORMATION

Perhaps the most God-like quality humans can acquire is truth. And arguably, the greatest promise the fallen human race has ever been given is the promise of 'all-truth'. This promise was given by Jesus, the Passover Lamb of God, the night before he shed his blood on Calvary. Fifty days later, on the Feast of Pentecost, the Holy Spirit would empower that promise.

From that moment, the biological clock of a new creation began ticking. Most would not sense it, or even care. Life is too demanding. Nevertheless, the promises of God, the work of the Spirit, have brought us to that harvest of all-truth. Today, if you choose, you the reader, can participate in the realization of this promise of a new world, created by humans, based on truth. This is our privilege!

The evidence is clear: mankind is on the verge of a cosmic transformation. The childhood world is about to give way to the adult world. Most of Biblical prophecy focuses on this transition. And yet, the details of this story are largely unknown—even by Christianity, which has the lead role.

But before we can have an adult world, we must learn adult ideas. These come slowly. But even in our recent history, we can see a quickening pace of reformation (truth coming).

Five hundred years ago social, spiritual, and theological pressures exploded in the form of a religious reformation. In 1517, a Catholic professor and priest, Martin Luther, wrote a paper describing his 'disputations' with some current religious practices. This paper was sent to church authority, and according to tradition was nailed to the door of All Saints' Church in Wittenberg, Germany. That paper has become known as Luther's Ninety-Five Theses.

The world was ready for change. Greatly supporting this change was the recent invention of the printing press (80 years earlier). Low-cost, mass distribution of new ideas was now possible. (Likewise, today we have the Internet, just in time.)

Three months later, friends of Luther translated the Ninety-Five Theses from Latin into German. Within two weeks, copies of the theses had spread throughout Germany. Within two months, they had spread throughout Europe. Soon, students thronged to Wittenberg to hear Luther speak.

These events have transformed Western Civilization for the better. But, as in most human affairs, they fell short of a full reformation. Prophecy, in particular, was not part of this theological reformation. Christian prophecy remains, even to this day, largely unresolved, being unable to adequately address many prophetic themes in a unified model.

Take for instance, 'oneness', another adult promise. Jesus prayed that his Body would be one: "*May they be brought to complete unity to let the world know...*" (John 17:23), and Paul: "*until we all reach unity in the faith...*" (Eph. 4:13). These are prophetic statements that have not yet come to fruition. Prophecies like these, are not part of traditional Christian apocalyptic prophecy. How these absolute prophecies are ultimately to be fulfilled cannot be explained by current Christian prophecy. Theological diversity (hundreds of denominations) is a symptom of prophetic confusion.

Continuing Reformation

Perhaps the greatest result of the first reformation was to set the Bible free, making it available to the common people. That freedom brought waves of subsequent reformations, even into the twenty-first century. But there is one reformation that has NOT happened yet—a PROPHETIC REFORMATION.

We can trace back the slow progression of 'truth-coming' 500 years. In that time, we have also seen the birth of America, great revivals, and worldwide evangelical campaigns. In the last one hundred years, we have witnessed such restorative highlights as the Pentecostal movement, the restoration of Israel, the Charismatic movement, and the Messianic movement.

This book will introduce the missing components of reformation, prophetic reformation, and tell the story of how these promised truths will transform humanity and the world. The universal prayer, *"Thy kingdom come..."* is truly a surprising story. The prophets of Israel gave us the outline, but we will discover it's up to us to write the final script. We challenge the reader to a serious discussion on 'how the kingdom comes!'

Finding a Prophetic Vocabulary

Biblical Prophecy can be a blizzard of confusing details. Oftentimes, it is non-systematically presented to us in Scripture. We must pursue a prophetic vocabulary by studying the Old Testament, and the spiritual history of mankind as recorded in the Bible. The New Testament writers used that vocabulary, added to it, and connected many of the dots in God's progressive work in history. We must try, as much as possible to frame prophetic details within their larger patterns.

The Division of Time

It is not insignificant that Genesis begins with the division of time—seven days. Thinking like God in this respect, managing and defining time units as a first prerequisite, we will do likewise.

Expanding on this pattern of the week, there are prophetically important units of time called millenniums. Let's take a quick look at how God speaks to us through millenniums.

Millennium Background

The prefix 'mille' means 1,000. A prophetic millennium is a period of (approximately) 1,000 years. It is quite evident that God is using millenniums, particularly a week of millenniums, as a prophetic framework for human history.

The 'week' is a significant prophetic structure. From the first chapter of the Bible we see this emphasis. God did it, and so, for...

> Six days YOU shall labor and do all YOUR work, but the seventh day is a Sabbath to the LORD your God. [Deuteronomy 5:13-14]

And so, God rested... The pattern of 'work' and 'rest' has been given to us from the beginning. Expanding on the week pattern, we learn from Scripture that 'a day equals a thousand years' (Psalm 90:4, 2 Peter 3:8). We will refer to this week of millenniums as the 'prophetic week'.

Abraham entered world history at the beginning of the third day; David and the Temple began the fourth day; and Jesus the Messiah began the fifth day. And the last 2,000 years are often referred to as 'the last days' (days five and six). What remains of the prophetic week is the seventh day, which has become commonly known as 'the Millennium'.

In the early Christian church, Hippolytus of Rome (170 – 235 AD), the most important 3rd-century theologian in Rome wrote:

> *"And 6,000 years must needs be accomplished, in order that the Sabbath may come, the rest, the holy day 'on which God rested from all His works.' For the Sabbath is the type and emblem of the future kingdom of the saints, when they 'shall reign with Christ,' when He comes from heaven, as John says in his Apocalypse: for 'a day with the Lord is as a thousand years.' Since, then, in six days God made all things, it follows that 6,000 -years must be fulfilled." (Hippolytus. On the HexaËmeron, Or Six Days' Work. From Fragments from Commentaries on Various Books of Scripture). [Millennialism - Wikipedia]*

Christian tradition supports a 7,000-year framework for human history. (Note the implied 'start' of the Millennium in the Hippolytus quote above is '*when He comes from heaven* '. From afar, this mistaken timing has little impact, but as we move closer to the start of the 'Sabbath' day (Millennium), this truth becomes critically important, as we will see soon.

Jewish tradition also frames human history within the prophetic week. From the Babylonian Talmud:

> *"It was taught in the School of Elijah, the [fallen Edenic] world will endure [exist] six thousand years – two thousand years in chaos [without law], two thousand years with Torah [with law], and two thousand years will be the days of the Messiah." (Tractate Sanhedrin, Folio 97a, as translated by A. Cohen in 'Everyman's Talmud', pg. 356) (Our brackets added for emphasis and clarity):*

Three dispensations of two-thousand years. It is so interesting that Jewish tradition, perhaps from the time of Elijah, believed that the fifth and the sixth millenniums would be the '*days of Messiah*'. Indeed, they have been.

The writer of Hebrews makes a distinction between earlier prophetic millenniums (one through four) and the fifth and sixth millenniums declaring:

> *"In the past [prophetic days 1-4] God spoke to our forefathers through the prophets at many times and in various ways, but in these last [two] days he has spoken to us by his Son..." Hebrews 1:1-2)*

It's not hard to see the writer of Hebrews could be paraphrasing the oral tradition from the Talmud quoted above, 'and two-thousand years will be the days of the Messiah.' The Messiah truly has spoken to us prophetically in these 'last days', particularly in regard to his disciples' participation in the seventh Millennium.

So, we see a millennium is a valid and vital prophetic concept to understand. The Bible, Christianity, Judaism, and human history promote the idea of a prophetic week as the basis for prophecy. And especially pertinent for us is the 'last millennium,' the Sabbath Millennium.

The Sabbath Millennium is not like all the rest. We have never had one of these before. It is not just a distinct unit of time. It has a unique function and unique rules. Just based on a proper understanding of time (6000+ years since Adam), we live in the days of a transition mankind has never seen before.

We learn from Genesis that God thinks and works in 'week' units. From a Biblical perspective, the Sabbath is the end of the work-week. So, human history appears to be at the end of its 'work-week' and near the beginning of 'rest'. How does this play out prophetically? This is the story we will share in greater detail throughout this book.

Thinking in terms of a 'week of millenniums' is essential to understanding prophecy. We will see, Jesus framed his only prophetic survey, Mathew 24, around this concept.

Prophetic Reformation Examples

When a Jew speaks of 'the end', as Jesus does in Mathew 24:14, he is most naturally speaking of 'the end' of the week. In his culture, his whole week is lived pointing to one thing, 'the end' of the work-week

(6 days) and the beginning of the next Sabbath. Jewish culture revolves around the Sabbath. Sabbath is God's symbol of 'rest'. It is a 'day' that represents the world to come, the kingdom—the epitome of God's goodness for mankind.

Again, Jesus uses the Sabbath Millennium as the framework for his prophecy message in Mathew 24. That message includes:

1) a 'testimony' about the coming Millennium
2) 'the end' of the sixth millennium
3) The start of the 'first generation' of the Millennium, and
4) the final expression of that mature 'first generation', before resurrection and Messiah's literal return to earth.

These concepts should be so natural and obvious, and they would be much more so, had Christianity not changed the rules. Today, Christian theology has no seventh day Sabbath. They have no 'end'… Or, do they?

To add to the confusion, ask a prophetically aware Christian what 'the end' is and they would have a much different answer than Jesus. Their 'end' would naturally point to the return of Jesus; the end of the world system without Jesus in control. For Christianity, 'the end' is the rapture and/or resurrection.

But the Bible doesn't refer to Messiah's coming as 'the end'. Quite the contrary in Mathew 24. Notice how Jesus refers to his 'second coming' (*'when he returns'*) in verse 46. 'The end' is in verse 14, the beginning of restoration, well before 'the return' in verse 45,46. 'The end' comes many decades before the *Joseph* ministry (verse 45), which is just before Jesus' return.

It will be good for that servant whose master [Jesus] finds him doing so <u>when he returns</u>. (Mathew 24:46)

We cannot resolve prophecy with confusion like this. These essential corrections will come with prophetic reformation.

Also, Paul framed his prophecy around the 'Feasts of the Lord', particularly the Exodus in Romans 8, another essential prophetic foundation. Again, Christianity changed the rules, they have no "Feasts of the Lord".

Based on current Christian culture, prophecy is undecipherable. It is not hard to see the need for prophetic reformation. Bad prophecy indicates bad theology. Good prophecy will correct bad theology.

More Vocabulary

This is why we have to work hard at creating a proper prophetic vocabulary. The prophecy in this book is so new it will require defining or redefining many terms and assigning terms to new concepts. This is a painful but necessary step. At times there may be a question of what to do first; assign the term or explain the concept. And many terms can only be understood when related to each other.

But there are a few terms we need to mention right up front to help us get started. We will add to this terminology in "MORE PROPHETIC VOCABULARY" in Chapter 7.

End-of-the-age

'End-of-the-age' is a Biblical term which has many variations throughout the OT and NT. Some of those are: 'end of the world', 'time of the end', 'last days', 'days to come' and 'in those days'. This term can be used in a general sense as a whole period, or a specific event as Jesus did when he referred to 'the end' in Matthew 24:14

Generally, end-of-the-age represents a special period of time, perhaps 50+ years long, that we also call the 'first generation' of the Millennium.

This may be confusing. While the end-of-the-age includes a single event, we (and Jesus) call 'the end', the majority of this period is actually the beginning of the next age, the Millennium.

This *restoration* period is the focal point of Biblical prophecy and this book. The general boundaries of this period are from the coming of 'Elijah' (Mark 9:12a) to the physical coming of Messiah. ['Elijah' probably does not mean 'Elijah the man' or even a single man. There is the 'spirit of Elijah', and there are many 'Elijahs', John the Baptist was one of them.]

Prophetic Model

We also use the term 'prophetic model' extensively. It simply means a systematic theory of God's purposes for mankind, etc., during the 'prophetic week' (7000 years). But more specifically, we use model to describe the sum total of the events and transformations that are part of the end-of-the-age. Including how the kingdom of God, how the government and the will of God, is actually manifested on earth. There are dozens, perhaps hundreds of prophetic models within Christianity and yet few if any describe in any detail how the kingdom is actually apprehended and/or imposed on humanity.

Restoration

'Restore' and 'restore all things' is a Biblical term that harkens back to the Garden of Eden with its image of a perfect paradise. By using the Garden paradise and sinlessness as a backdrop, it helps us put this idea of 'restore' its proper context.

Restoration is the process and initial activity needed to reorder the world according to kingdom principles. It is the legal and governmental reordering of human culture and institutions in preparation for the formal administration of Messiah in the Millennium. Full *Restoration* is the ministry of '*Elijah*' and '*Joseph*' 'preparing the way'.

In our context, the 'end-of-the-age' and '*Restoration*' may often be used synonymously. 'End-of-the-age' is the period, and '*Restoration*' is the purpose or activity of that period. Again, we will add to this in "MORE PROPHETIC VOCABULARY" in Chapter 7.

Millennium Commissions

No example of the distinction between 'childhood thinking' verses 'adult thinking' is clearer than the example of the Millennium commissions in Mathew 24. As illustrated in Appendix A: One Question: A Personal-Discovery Exercise, when the exercise is read as a child listening to a parent, we take away a certain message. Generally, we will find that message in Christian commentaries. When the exercise is read as 'ministers' 'seeking first the kingdom' we will take away a much different message—the intended message. Essentially, the two major commissions in it pop out at us and we begin to fit all the supporting prophetic pieces around them. (If you haven't read Appendix A: One Question: A Personal-Discovery Exercise you should do so now.)

We can see by this, that the Millennium commissions are not so much hidden prophecy, as they indicate a prophetic identity not previously engaged. Resolving this exercise does not require revelation as much as it requires maturity. And that idea itself, becoming mature, is a prophetic concept as well. The commissions have remained undeciphered because of Christianity's childhood perceptions and traditions.

Mankind has experienced childhood with its spiritual limitations. Deciphering the Millennium commissions prove that the sons of God are ready to be revealed, ready to take on a new role as adult. We have struggled through childhood, but with the guiding hand of the Holy Spirit we have now begun to think as adult sons of God.

How it Begins

As this prophecy becomes clear, one of the big surprises we learn is how the Millennium begins. Traditionally, the Millennium starts with the literal return of Messiah (Jesus) to earth. But you will soon discover that this idea is incorrect. This belief is actually one of those childhood ideas that inhibits the fulfilment of the Millennium.

The Millennium commissions, as revealed by Jesus, reveal something quite different. We will see that the Millennium starts, not with the return of Jesus, but with the 'return' of **Adam** and a special generation who bring a worldwide *Restoration*. The sons of God must initiate and manage this period.

This is not an academic exercise; it is deadly serious. The Millennium (or Kingdom) is the only answer to the world's many troubles. God's intention and his promise is that mankind will finally enjoy a world of righteousness, peace, and prosperity. It is a 'Sabbath rest' that will eventually bring an end to violence, injustice, disease, pain, suffering, and eventually death. Do you take that seriously enough?

According to the Bible, the whole universe is eagerly waiting to see this promise fulfilled. And this Kingdom must begin well before the return of the King. Resolving these mysteries will unlock blessings for all mankind.

Here is an important truth to understand. The King is coming TO a kingdom, not to START a kingdom. A true (Biblical) king does not coronate himself; he does not impose his kingdom on his subjects. His kingship is a product of his subjects will; their call to make him king.

The Spirit and the bride say, "Come!" (Rev 22:17)

We will tell that story in greater detail, but emerging from the first generation of the Millennium, there will come three MATURE people groups. This is a required PREPARATION, BEFORE Messiah RETURNS as King.

The Challenge

Man caused the trouble to this earth, and man must be deeply involved in resolving the problem. That is what Jesus says in Matthew 24. The

Millennium is ultimately about people and government. Jesus' words point his disciples to a framework in which that will happen.

We have a serious challenge: As Jesus said, "If you love me, you will [discover and] keep my commands!" Above all, that includes his prophetic commands—there is no one else to do this. Our duty begins with deciphering the Millennium commissions. Deciphering the commissions is fulfilling the commissions!

This Book

This book is divided into two sections. They are independent yet complimentary. They could be read in reverse order if the reader wishes.

Section One: PROPHETIC REFORMATION

Section 1, highlights the product of the author's more recent prophetic study. It is generally about ideas and/or theology explaining how Christianity must transform itself and prepare for its prophetic ministry.

Chapter 1 chronicles the high points of five-hundred years of reformation culminating with prophetic 'all truth' (effectively, The Millennium commissions—the only framework for a prophetic model).

Chapters 3, 4, and 5, outline a framework for the necessary internal transformation of Christian ministry.

Section Two: THE PROPHETIC STORY OF MANKIND

Section 2, is generally about the process, the past and future of mankind's prophetic journey leading to a new kingdom order.

It is directed specifically toward the prophetic events nearest at hand. Section two gives an overview of how the nations, families and governments of earth, are literally reset to kingdom principles.

God, through his prophets, will conquer earth with supernatural power. Mankind will know the one true God. Essentially, the second Edenic start will come with God 'walking' in the garden again.

This book is not meant to present detailed arguments to many of the theological points used in the overview. There needs to be more documents written to complete the systematic theology supporting the prophetic model introduced here. Future presentations will have to be more apologetic in tone and provide more in-depth explanations of some of the key issues.

Appendixes

Appendix A: is a Personal-Discovery Exercise mentioned in the Introduction. The full prophecy model of this book is centered on elements from Jesus' prophetic sermon in Mathew 24. If you want to discover those key elements for yourself you can do this exercise before reading the book.

Appendix B: presents the prophetic model in a number of succinct summary lists that help to clarify the larger story. They can be used as reference notes.

It is very likely you have not heard a story like this—positive prophecy. It should be a griping and intriguing read. Together, the sections chart the course and the actions needed to restore this world and its people to the glory intended.

One Last Note

In various places we make summary statements similar to the one below:

> *Through prophetic wisdom, God's prophetic ministry will declare, once again, and even greater: 'Peace on earth goodwill to men'. They will preach the 'gospel of the kingdom' and trigger the Millennium. They will conquer this world and restore righteous foundations to a born-again universe.*

This is written in the 'positive' tenor of this whole book, which is always the best approach. However, it is fully recognized that a restoration coming at the very start of the Millennium, and the virtually exclusive subject of this book, will be short lived. It is recognized, though not dealt with in this book, that the Biblical 'falling away' or 'rebellion' (2 Thessalonians 2:3), and the 'Antichrist incident' that most prophecy dwells on, will briefly interrupt the positive, peaceful, restorative nature of the 1000-year Millennium.

This is intentional. The 'falling away' cannot be understood properly unless the full *Restoration*, the subject of this book, is successfully implemented first. Only with the 'kingdom conquest' event described in this book can this 'anti' period ('falling away') be understood. There will be plenty of time to properly describe those periods which come many decades in the future. So, they are not dealt with here.

Chapter Two

COSMIC IDENTITY

This book highlights the many deficiencies of current Christian theology and prophecy. In a very real sense, Christianity stands at the same place as the wilderness generation—in-between Egypt and the Promised Land.

In our childhood bubble we have unconsciously avoided many adult realities. Take for instance, spiritual songs about the river (Jordan). The River Jordan is an important station in the Biblical journey from Egypt to the Promised Land. We will see later, the journey is THE framework for the prophetic end-of-the-age.

However, in our current spiritual culture, the Promised Land (across the river) is virtually always depicted as 'heaven' (after death). Here is one song, "Michael row the boat ashore":

Michael row the boat ashore, Hallelujah!
Michael row the boat ashore, Hallelujah!
Jordan's river is deep and wide, hallelujah.
Meet my mother on the other side, hallelujah.

Michael is the archangel Michael. It is believed that Michael helps ferry souls of the dead to heaven.

Another popular song depicting the Promised Land as heaven is, "Because He lives" (Bill and Gloria Gaither). (This song was one of six personally picked by Billy Graham to be sung at his funeral).

> *(v4) And then one day*
> *I'll cross the river,*
> *I'll fight life's final war with pain;*
> *And then as death gives way to victory,*
> *I'll see the lights of glory and*
> *I'll know he lives.*

Why is 'across the Jordan' an almost universal metaphor for heaven? Yes, it feels so right. Of course, our Promised Land is heaven! (it is assumed). Christianity has many things that just feel right, but they are often childhood fantasies or much less than the whole truth.

It is true that (true) Christians are citizens of heaven, but the real Biblical Promised Land contained seven enemy nations. The real story is that after 'crossing the river' Israel had to be circumcised, have a Passover, and fight its way in (seven+ years) before it had rest.

Childhood stories work. They are good for a season. They are simple and popular. They can add so much at bedtime or around the fireplace. But... they are seldom the adult story. The adult story has an Egypt, a wilderness, a Jordan river, and a Promised Land. It's good to be familiar with all the challenges of the journey story.

One can speculate that the people of Israel, upon leaving Egypt, never anticipated their long 40 year journey in the wilderness, either. They were headed to their Promised Land, 'What, with God's help, perhaps several weeks journey', they may have thought. Little did they know the transformation that would be required of them in their journey.

This 'foreshortening' of the journey is quite natural (and perhaps even necessary) in human societies. Christianity has done the same with their 'Promised Land' (the return of Jesus). The 'imminent return' is the leading prophetic view of Christian society today. This 'imminent return' view has virtually no concept of the Biblical 'preparing the way', the subject of this book (*Restoration*).

So, there is a very fine line between childhood and faithlessness. The Book of Hebrews uses this very journey story to warn us of this tendency to ignore painful truths. Let's build a short montage from several chapters in Hebrews.

> *2:1 We must pay more careful attention, therefore, to what we have heard, so that we do not drift away.*
>
> *3:7 So, as the Holy Spirit says: "Today, if you hear his voice, 8 do not harden your hearts as you did in the rebellion, during the time of testing in the desert, 9 where your fathers tested and tried me and for forty years saw what I did. 10 That is why I was angry with that generation, and I said, 'Their hearts are always going astray, and they have not known my ways.' 11 So I declared on oath in my anger, 'They shall never enter my rest.'"*
>
> *3:16 Who were they who heard and rebelled? Were they not all those Moses led out of Egypt?*
>
> *4:6 It still remains that some will enter that rest, and those who formerly had the gospel preached to them did not go in, because of their disobedience.*
>
> *4:9 There remains, then, a Sabbath-rest for the people of God;*

Let's repeat what we said earlier. In a very real sense, Christianity stands at the same place as the wilderness generation; in-between Egypt and the Promised Land. [It's interesting that using a Jubilee measure (49 years) to calculate one year, Christianity has literally been in the 'wilderness' 40 years.]

In short, Christianity has substituted the goal of conquering the 'Promised Land' with 'going to the Promised Land' (heaven). Effectively saying, 'how can we possibly conquer those giants'?

In, *'being more careful'*, we have to ask ourselves, who are we, really? The Christian church (and by that we mean the true Body of Christ), has an identity crisis that has wide ranging implications. Not understanding who we are, has greatly affected our perception of our goals, and the means to those goals here on earth.

In short, we have not understood the magnitude of our own promised transformation as part of our identity, and therefore our God given role in management of earth and creation.

Struggling with Identity

How can we explain this? How can we explain our (Christianity's) failure to see our call to these 'greater works'? Finding one's identity and purpose is a struggle. It comes neither quick or easy. And often it must be preceded by discovering who we are not.

God brought order into creation via separation (division). Separating light from darkness, water from earth, six days from the seventh. Division is an important step in discovering one's intended identity. Imagine Adam's sense of identity before, and after, he was divided into male and female.

Sometimes the whole cannot find its identity because there are really two identities appearing as one. In this case division is necessary.

Another confusing element in our search for identity, are the stages of childhood and adulthood. A critical step toward adulthood is the realization one is not a child any longer. Even this is a struggle and not instantaneous.

These natural and necessary phases of development need to be understood. As we said earlier, humanity is about to enter the adult world. But we must realize that can only happen when God has adult partners. Human partners, who themselves become aware of adult truth, and take on the role of adult managers. The whole creation is waiting for this 'revealing'.

There is a certain unsophisticated dignity in being a child. It is a time of childhood truths and childhood behavior often noted for its purity and innocence. But childhood is never the destination, and childhood truth is never enough. We can see Jesus invoked this childhood/adulthood language in his Upper Room Discourse (John 14-

17). This sermon is so important to the issues discussed here and below that it could be thought of as our 'Identity Sermon'.

> "I have much more to say to you, more than you can now bear [in childhood]. But when he, the Spirit of truth, comes, he will guide you into all truth [adulthood]. (John 16: 12-13)

After 2000 years of the Spirit's work, do we dare standup and say, yes, we are ready for adult truth and all the implications that may bring? This is the impetus for prophetic reformation. To bring healing, order and reconciliation, an adult service (beyond salvation), to the world.

Perhaps the first step is to think through how adult truth is different than childhood truth?

In childhood, 'obedience' largely consists of 'doing what we are told'. It is a time of learning boundaries, principles, and compliance. A time of close supervision and instruction. Creative self-initiative, or thinking for yourself, is not preeminent at this stage.

But the passive obedience stage gives way to principled initiative in the adult world. Learned righteousness now is directed into forceful initiative. As we discover a world less than complete, less than perfect, we ask, "How can wrongs be righted, how can goodness be multiplied?" An adult now looks to find his place and purpose in overcoming deficiencies and creating a better world.

A well-formed adult redirects the natural urges of pleasure, ambition, and glory-seeking into the purposes of God as he understands them. Now the emphasis changes from 'doing what we are told' to discerning the inner voice of the Spirit of God and letting that Spirit direct our lives. Love, motivates not a command driven life, but a passion to fulfill the unspoken desires of the beloved, our heavenly Father. This kind of creative human initiative is what glorifies God.

As any loving couple knows, this type of unspoken 'obedience' is the most meaningful. As we learn creative obedience, we begin to see God's intentions for this world; for the adult world yet to come. It must be born out of this kind of creative human initiative. It must be born out of love, not command. We will see how that is realized in other sections of this book.

This 'becoming adult' is a well-recognized rite in Judaism. They recognize this important social construct with a special observance called a Bar Mitzvah. A child becomes a man, or more specifically, "an [agent] who is [now] subject to the law".

An adult world is a world with new legal privileges and responsibilities. Toward the end of this discussion we will discuss three goals of prophetic reformation; effectively three legal directives; new adult directives. They are: 1) defining a prophetic model, 2) Christianity's internal reordering, and 3) the final testimony of a new legal charter. But first let's develop a little more background for those goals.

Cosmic Responsibility

Do you, the reader and member of the Body of Christ, understand your (corporate) responsibility toward this earth? What is that responsibility beyond evangelism?

For instance, do you believe there is a (temporary) curse upon creation because of mankind's (Adam's) sin? If so, how, and when will it be lifted? How will this affect earth and its people? What benefit would that have for humans? Is this an important goal for you? Should it be?

As an example: one of the prominent terms the Bible uses to announce this creation changing (ending the curse) event is 'the gospel-of-the-kingdom'. And perhaps the first succinct statement of this gospel is found in Isaiah 40:

> *"Comfort, comfort my people, says your God. Speak tenderly to Jerusalem, and proclaim to her that her hard service has been completed, that her sin has been paid for, that she has received from the Lord's hand double for all her sins. A voice of one calling: "In the desert prepare the way for the Lord; make*

straight in the wilderness a highway for our God. Every valley shall be raised up, every mountain and hill made low; the rough ground shall become level, the rugged places a plain. And the glory of the Lord will be revealed, and all mankind together will see it. For the mouth of the Lord has spoken." (Isaiah 40:1-5)

Here, '*speak tenderly to Jerusalem*' is a specific statement to Jerusalem, Israel and the Jewish people. But the larger context reveals it is also a message directed to '*all mankind together*'. The passage describes a transition; the ending of one world dispensation, and the beginning of the next.

Is this event accounted for in current Christian prophecy? Not hardly. Ideas central to both Jesus' (Mathew 24:14) and Paul's (Romans 8: 18-21) prophecy statements are found in the passage above, but they are not part of any leading Christian prophecy models. We will examine this passage in greater detail later; how the ending of '**hard service**' is a major, yet uncharted, event in the Christian prophetic story.

This is just to illustrate the need for prophetic reformation. Due to a childlike simplicity in our theology, very few people will understand the issues discussed above. We are warned about staying childlike and elementary too long.

"How long, ye simple ones, will ye love simplicity? (Proverbs 1:22);

You need milk, not solid food! (Hebrews 5:12) (A chastisement)

Understanding how we master this new adult world will require a radical new understanding of who we are and the larger task of reconciliation, God has ordained for us. Jesus taught us to pray…

"your kingdom come, your will be done on earth as it is in heaven." (Matthew 6:10)

But this prayer has become rote. How many connect this with the gospel-of-the-kingdom (Isaiah 40) mentioned above, and expect to be part of, or really pray for, its fulfilment?

Our adult priority is not going to heaven but restoring the earth; the kingdom on earth; God's will on earth. That process must include repairing our own fallenness with the grace and truth provided, but then we must bless the nations of earth.

We have forgotten man's first responsibility. He, Adam, (now us) was placed in the garden (now the world) to serve it and protect it (Genesis 2:15). We have been given *the ministry of reconciliation:* (2 Corinthians 5:18).

Understanding the Coming of Truth - Reformation

These truths should be at the heart of Christian prophecy, but they are not. The progressive work of reformation has prepared and equipped believers with a greater understanding of God and his truth. The Messianic movement in particular has brought a mega-shift in Christian theology not seen in 2000 years, although to only a relatively small segment of Christianity so far.

Sanctify them by the Truth

Nevertheless, the basis for Messianic theology has been thoroughly studied and resolved. New documents have been written, and tens of thousands of believing Christians (Jew and Gentile) are participating in a worship style more authentic in theology and practice. A Christianity devoid of its Hebraic roots is clearly no longer theologically defensible (except by Christian tradition), nor was it practiced by Christianity's early apostolic Fathers.

A 'law-less', non-Judaic, Christianity can be defended as an early accommodation to a pagan gentile world, but it cannot be defended as 'adult' and complete theology. Yeshua (Jesus) never taught these

Pauline accommodations to 'the twelve'. Yes, it has been difficult and confusing at times, but rightly understood and resolved, we can now look back and see the need and the roles of both 'childhood' and 'adult' kingdom theology.

The truth is sanctifying us. A major aspect of this new wind is a clearer understanding of the 'goal' and 'structure' of the coming kingdom, and our responsibility in bringing it about.

The 'end-game' requires a new honesty and introspection regarding truth. A passion for truth (reality) is the heritage of the people of God; it always has been. But truth is not necessarily what we've always done or believed. Each generation is confronted with the struggle to balance truth and tradition. Ideally, they are the same, but history testifies that's rarely the case. There is clear evidence that our traditions have been less than ideal.

It is time for mainstream Christianity, true Christianity, to recognize and confess the sins of our fathers, and that certain elements of theological error (often half-truths) have become part of our traditions and institutions.

We needn't get unduly judgmental about this. God's sovereign work has been, and will continue to be, accomplished in spite of man's failures. Even man's failures are positively included in God's sovereign purposes. The world has been transformed by the simple Christian gospel of salvation. But a truly contrite humility would be a great asset in the challenging journey to define all the elements of reformation.

This journey to all-truth is both a promise, and a responsibility. The truth Scripture again...

But when he, the Spirit of truth, comes, he will guide you into all truth. He will not speak on his own; he will speak only what he hears, and he will tell you what is yet to come. (John 16:13)

Notice the connection between 'all-truth' and 'yet to come' (prophecy). That is no coincidence. Prophecy is the path, the only path, to all-truth. Resolved prophecy is the preeminent evidence of all-truth.

Looking Back

To discover who we are we must look back to the garden of Eden. Man was made in the image of God and he was assigned the responsibility to manage creation. Sadly, and we know the story, Adam sinned.

God, as a loving parent, responded; *'creation was subjected to frustration'* (Romans 8:20). Today it is clear—through Adam, *"all have sinned and fallen short of the glory (or image) of God* (Romans 3:23).

Paradise on earth was deferred, but not abandoned, we are promised. This detour, though hard, will bring even greater good. Now begins a new story, remarkably, part of which we must write ourselves, and carry out.

Creation has been frustrated, yes, but even that can work for good. The greatest tragedy would be to lose sight of what it means to restore paradise on earth. Unfortunately, that is the case today. Christianity has substituted 'salvation', and 'going to heaven' for the highest goal of 'seeking first the kingdom' and 'ending creation's frustration'.

Our Highest Hope

We could sum up the highest goal as the 'hope of the glory of God' (in us). First salvation; but salvation is not as an end in itself. Salvation gives us access to 'the hope'. Here are Paul's words…

> *Therefore, since we have been justified through faith, we have peace with God through our Lord Jesus Christ, through whom we have gained access by faith into this grace in which we now stand. And we rejoice in the hope of the glory of God. (Romans 5:1-2)*

Today, our highest hope is regaining the 'glory of God'—restoring the reality of our fundamental identity lost in Eden. This is the only mantle from which we have access to our responsibility. Responsibility to return order to this world. There is no other program other than our success.

What we (Christianity) believe about prophecy is not optional, its strategic. Summing up this failure into a comprehensible package, we could say it is a failure to understand 'truth'. For our purposes here, we'll define truth as 'reality', 'that which is the case, rather than that which is assumed'. This failure is the most serious outcome of the 'fall' in Eden. This is where prophetic reformation must begin—overcoming this flaw in the current human condition. This is Paul's conclusion:

> *Do not conform any longer to the pattern of this world, but be transformed by the renewing of your mind. Then you will be able to test and approve what God's will is--his good, pleasing and perfect will. (Romans 12:2)*

Renewing your mind. This is not an 'avoid evil' statement. This is a 'death to self' statement. Death to one good identity, in favor of a higher identity. Stop for a moment and think about it. What are 'patterns of this world'? Fundamentally, Paul is NOT directly talking about 'evil' things or patterns here. He is talking about 'good things' that can oppose 'perfect things'. Jesus also talked about the 'cares of the world' like this.

Let me ask you, what is perhaps the ultimate 'pattern of this world'? You probably didn't consider the one I am about to mention—marriage (1Co 7:33). Marriage is 'worldly' in a prophetic sense. Think of all the other 'worldly' things—family, children, work, education, entertainment, that could hinder us from our highest hope!

Our Greatest Enemy

Evil is not our greatest enemy—childhood is. Our greatest enemy is not perceiving the greatest reality. It is the 'good' things of earth that largely obstruct God's highest prophetic ends. As citizens of heaven we may be called to deny the goodness of earth, embracing a new (seemingly foreign) identity.

Christian Ministry

Try to summarize Christianity's current ministry to mankind. We could say that Christianity has elevated to its highest purpose 'salvation' and 'living', both vital ministries. But is this our highest responsibility? Is this a remedy for the fall? Only indirectly. Salvation and living are major concerns for humans, but according to Scripture, they are not supposed to be our FIRST concern.

As sons of God and citizens of heaven, literally, who have been legally charged with judging angels (spiritual realms) and managing creation, our first objective must be truth (understanding creation as it truly is). That is something humanity does not have today. Imagine agents in charge of a project not understanding the true nature of that project?

Let's force ourselves to put *Restoration* in more specific terms. Can you, yourself, (or Christianity) describe, 'how does the kingdom come to earth, in detail'? Do you understand the events, the process, that will impose the kingdom on seven billion people? What kind of government, laws, and culture will be required to maintain a just and peaceful world? How would you coerce billions of people to live within a kingdom culture? Do you know?

This is especially important for us today as we formulate a detailed model of the end of-the-age. If we, in fact, are the agents assigned to bring this about, one can see the importance of truth. Christianity today is not equipped to implement the kingdom on earth. The question would be asked, "which Christianity?" (there are thousands) or "which laws?"

Nevertheless, we must remember God's promises. They include, all-truth, all-power, all-love, and oneness (all adult promises). One can see that knowing reality (truth) is critical. And we contend, that resolving the prophetic program going forward IS the highest evidence of knowing reality.

This kingdom responsibility has not flowered in the Christian mindset. Regardless, this apprehension of truth is the final and essential goal of Christianity in the end-times (before resurrection). In the human story, we have reached the time of these new demands.

This promised (even demanded) destination is encapsulated in the Biblical notions of kingdom, *Restoration*, conforming to Christ, and perfection. In Jesus' words: '*seek first the kingdom*' and '*(the Holy Spirit) will lead you into all truth*'.

Beyond Salvation

Acquiring truth is not the automatic outcome of 'salvation'. Truth must be acquired deliberately and forcefully. In one sense, acquiring truth might be thought of as a 'second salvation'. Truth must be the fruit of salvation. Truth, will indeed, set us, and indirectly, all of humanity, free.

Transitions like this are declared, and initially directed, by a special ministry given to the Body called the prophetic ministry. Not coincidentally, the prophetic ministry is a truth ministry. Its priorities are truth first, rather than the current (complimentary) 'salvation and living' priority.

In the big scheme of things, THERE IS NOTHING MORE IMPORTANT than the 'sons' perceiving, and then acting upon these stated goals. The apostle Paul could not state it more sublimely,

> *I consider that our present sufferings are not worth comparing with the glory that will be revealed in us. THE CREATION waits in eager expectation for the sons of God to be revealed. (Romans 8:18-19)*

He seems to be saying, 'creation waits for us!' Creation? Really? Do you ever think in those terms?

Life goes on; the cares of life issue demands, but we cannot, we dare not, trivialize or ignore these most lofty Biblical demands. Today's Christian doctrine (truth) is sufficient to get people to heaven, but it is not sufficient to get the kingdom of heaven to earth.

Making the Transition

This complex transition to a truth-based (or kingdom implementing) priority, will require great faith and effort.

For the *"kingdom to come, and God's will on earth to be done"*, Christianity must transition toward a prophetic administration brought about by a prophetic reformation; rebuilding our theology, eschatology, and thinking, based on the truths highlighted here is the only solution.

If we summarize the basic targets of reformation, they would include three critical areas in the near term:

- **A New Prophetic Model** – Defining a written, legal model describing how the kingdom will be implemented on earth. (a mostly internal process)
- **A New Prophetic Order** – Advancing a corrective, legal, separation-of-powers (apostle and prophet) ministerial order within Christianity, that will bring an unprecedented release of adult truth and power
- **A New Prophetic Gospel** – Preparing the final truth and power testimony of the one true God, given to the world before 'the end', called the gospel-of-the-kingdom (an external prophetic evangelism)

Model, Order, Gospel—remember those three targets of reformation. They are new and they are directly connected to 'who we are', and 'our role' in kingdom bringing. We'll address each in more detail in the next three chapters.

Chapter Three

A NEW PROPHETIC MODEL

Defining a Written, Legal, Model

The Movie

If a movie were made depicting the end-of-the-age, one possible title, in today's language, might be "Reboot"—a 'reboot' of the human story. It would show a new Eden-like beginning for mankind within the context of the modern, established world of seven-plus billion people. Effectively, the beginning of a new world-order.

No, not an Antichrist world-order, so much of Christian prophecy is obsessed with, but a kingdom world-order declared by the prophets of Israel long ago. *"And the glory of the Lord will be revealed, and all mankind together will see it."* (Isaiah 40:1-5). The fulfilment of the prayers of billions of people when they pray, *"Thy kingdom come..."*. A kingdom of righteousness, peace and joy that this book discusses in some detail; that kingdom.

And, just for the record, we do acknowledge that there will be an Antichrist rebellion somewhere in the distant future (at the end of the first generation). But that should have very low priority, especially considering the poor understanding of the task WE are responsible for.

Adam

Looking back now, we can see Eden was the beginning of the childhood world, and the end-of-the-age will usher in the beginning of the adult world. And while Adam was generally a passive participant in forming the first world, the new '**Adam**', the Body of Christ, or the sons of God, (we will refer to this special **Adam** repeatedly), must take the lead in forming the new world. An adult **Adam** must be the lead 'craftsman' in creating his adult world.

In Messiah, men have become sons of God. But they have not truly operated in that identity until now. God, through the Holy Spirit, has invested greatly in the preparation of the sons of God. The intention and the goal is that they become like their redeemer, Christ. That they be conformed to the image of the Son (Romans 8:29). This is not just a theological notion. It is literally how the life of Christ will be manifested on earth (well before his literal return).

We may not understand the relevance of this idea. In the Identity Sermon Jesus says this:

> *"I am the vine; you are the branches. If a man remains in me and I in him, he will bear much fruit; apart from me you can do nothing. (John 15:5)*

Our dependence on Jesus is absolute, no question. However, (and this principle of inter-dependence is HUGE) the verse also implies that without us, Jesus has no fruit. The vine bears no fruit of itself, only the branches do. Think about that. That thinking is so contrary to much of the Christian world.

Adam is taking on the promised virtues of Messiah promised in the Identity Sermon. Conforming to his likeness—all-love, all-truth, all-power, and all the other attributes of an adult son. To what end? Preaching the gospel of salvation? No! That gospel has been effectively preached for 2000 years. That gospel (of going to heaven) is nearly over (just one last great harvest).

It is time for adult service, the service of restoring the earth through righteous government. That is truly God's business now. And, once again, this *Adam* is ordained to literally take over that business. Notice these Scriptures (again in the Identity Sermon):

I no longer call you servants, because a servant does not know his master's business. Instead, I have called you friends [brothers], for everything that I learned from my Father I have made known to you. (John 15:15)

and...

I tell you the truth, anyone who has faith in me will do what I have been doing. He will do even greater things than these, because I am going to the Father. (John 14:12)

Preaching to individuals about a personal, inner transformation (being born-again) is one thing, but creating a new world-order for seven billion people is quite a different thing.

Creating a new world-order, a reboot of world government, by *Adam* is a radically foreign concept, especially by Christianity who only sees a one world government (anytime soon) created by the Antichrist, and later Jesus when he returns.

The Script

So, how would man (*Adam*) demonstrate that he is truly ready to manage God's business; to do greater works than Jesus? Well, using our movie illustration above, he would write a script for "Reboot". The script would detail the process; the events and actions of how the kingdom is literally implemented on earth. It would commission *Adam* with remarkable power, tempered with divine wisdom and meekness.

This is something the world has never seen before. *Adam's* actions would not be driven by power, greed, ego, or rebellion. And while he is the driving force, the movie itself, is derived from someone else's 'Book'. The plot and process did not originate with him, nor is it even directly shaped for his benefit.

By going into the 'wilderness', *Adam* denies, even renounces, the earthly goodness for himself, now motivated only to bless the earth for others. *Adam* is a citizen of heaven, working for the benefit of earth.

Rather, he is an agent of peace, an anointed prophet. He would take the many discrete pieces of prophecy scattered throughout Scripture and create an actual production consistent with the Word of God. As in the Parable of the Talents (Mathew 25), he will draw on what he has been given directly (five talents) and through the creative Spirit (of Christ) within, produce a complete production (ten talents). In this way he would write a screenplay depicting the detailed story of how the kingdom can be (will be) implemented on earth.

This is fulfilling the adult challenge. Drawing on Scripture and history, man has been given the means to know God. The Holy Spirit has been guiding us to all-truth; to think and act like God. Just as a spouse learns the intimate ways of their partner, and a son learns from his father, man is ready to follow in his Father's footsteps. As the childhood world ends, *Adam* must first write the script detailing the re-creation of a new world.

Speech – A Creative Force

Our imaginary script is more than just a cute illustration. Part of man's management responsibility is to speak prophetically. Prophecy, speech, is a creative device. This is one of the laws of creation. We are learning what it means to become like God. God teaches us the mystical idea that words create.

Sanctify them by the truth; your word is truth. (John 17:17)

Right from the beginning we see that God spoke, and it became reality.

And God said, "Let there be light," and there was light. (Gen 1:3)

Since God has legally entrusted management of the world to man, God depends on man to drive his prophetic purposes. When there are men like Abraham, Moses and David available, mankind ascends. When there are none, humanity reverts. Through righteous action, linked with prophetic speech, the story of mankind progresses.

Our imaginary script is declaring in words what will soon become reality. This is required; this is how God works in history. The prophets of Israel have declared future reality. Much has already been fulfilled, even more has yet to be fulfilled. The kingdom cannot come unless it is declared (spoken) first.

Can we begin to understand the importance of prophetic reformation; the importance of truth? What we all long for is the adult world (whether we know it or not). To prove we are ready for that world we must describe that world, and how it must come, first.

We may think that Bible prophecy is just another kind of written history. That these accounts of discipline, judgement, or promise, are just written for our edification. We greatly benefit by these written records, but there is much more to them than that. These were legal declarations by man giving God the legal right to bring fulfilment.

Creating the Future

Authoritative prophecy is not just foretelling the future, it is creating the future. We may have overlooked this role of human initiative in Biblical history. Notice these Scriptures:

Now all this was done, that it might be fulfilled which was spoken of the Lord by the prophet, saying, (Mathew 1:22 KJV)

All this was done, that it might be fulfilled which was spoken by the prophet, saying, (Mathew 21:4 KJV)

I was daily with you in the temple teaching, and ye took me not: but the scriptures must be fulfilled. (Mark 14:49 KJV)

Dozens of times in the New Testament we have a phrase similar to this: "*that it might be fulfilled which was spoken by the prophet*". The prophet's words were not just informational, they were creative and legal.

With prophecy, God is not just showing us that he knows the future. No, in effect, God is saying (from Mathew 21:4 above), "The prophet has declared that Jesus would enter Jerusalem riding on a donkey. Today, I am legally fulfilling his words". Motivated by the Spirit within, the prophet had scripted how Jesus would enter Jerusalem, here it was legally fulfilled.

This is the case for our role today, to write a script or model of the adult world to come. The prophetic model will be legally binding. We have been given five pieces (the words of the prophets of Israel) and we will have to supply the remaining five, secrets of the kingdom, based upon the Spirit within and our knowledge of God's ways and his patterns. That God would honor man in this way, requiring his participation, shows God's remarkable goodness and grace.

Thus saith the LORD, the Holy One of Israel, and his Maker, Ask me of things to come concerning my sons, and concerning the work of my hands command ye me. (Isa 45:11 KJV)

Prophetic Reformation is necessary to understand and write the script for a new world-order. And that script must start with a new prophetic model. That model must include a new prophetic order.

Chapter Four

A NEW PROPHETIC ORDER

Advancing a Corrective Ministerial Order

The Next Big Thing—Restoring the Power

Who does not know someone who is desperately sick or physically suffering today? Suffering and hardship is part of the '**hard service**' of this age, but as children of God, we regularly intercede for supernatural deliverance for ourselves and others. Supernatural power is part of our heritage.

The question of (miraculous) power is perhaps the foremost prophetic issue confronting the Body of Messiah today. This age will not end without a promised, unprecedented, testimony of truth and power. Prophecy predicts the power floodgates are about to open. But we have to ask ourselves, how?

Legal power is evidence of intimacy with God. It must be included in the final testimony given to the world called the gospel-of-the-kingdom. But there must be great changes within the Body before this kind of power can be managed properly. We will now explore this critical issue of power, and its requisite companion, truth, and how it will return to the Body.

Virtually all Bible stories have a miraculous or supernatural element to them. The faithful are encouraged to ask God for power to effect miraculous healing, provision, and deliverance. The Christian ministry, in part, is an intercessory (priestly) ministry drawing from the supernatural for the sake of the needy.

In the Biblical record, demonstrations of supernatural power have brought kings, nations, and individuals to repentance. And yet, this power was dispensed judiciously and selectively. Special agents were anointed for very focused encounters at limited times. Having authority to dispense this power of God was a sign of favor or intimacy with God.

It seems apparent that God's intention is to give men, his 'sons', greater and greater, perhaps eventually absolute, access to this power. This should not surprise us. It is the proper heritage of a son— managing the Fathers resources, maturely. This was demonstrated in the gospel-of-the-kingdom testified to by Jesus and the apostles:

> *God also testified to it [the gospel-of-the-kingdom] by signs, wonders and various miracles, and gifts of the Holy Spirit distributed according to his will. It is not to angels that he has subjected the world to come, about which we are speaking. But there is a place where someone has testified: "What is man that you are mindful of him, the son of man that you care for him? You made him a little lower than the angels; you crowned him with glory and honor and put everything under his feet. In putting everything under him, God left nothing that is not subject to him. Yet at present we do not see everything subject to him. (Hebrews 2:4-8)*

The Preachers

As we have noted earlier, this final testimony of truth and power is the gospel-of-the-kingdom. The true Body of Yeshua was called and equipped to give this final testimony. It's in our DNA. We grew up hearing stories of our spiritual heroes raising the dead, stopping the sun, walking on water, and providing supernatural food. Healing the sick and casting out demons seemed commonplace in the first generation of the church. But for 2000 years the gospel message has become almost exclusively faith-based. God has been at work in much quieter ways.

The convicting work of the Holy Spirit with occasional, even rare, demonstrations of the supernatural, was enough to transform a pagan world. Faith has been our banner.

However, the inner (invisible) transformation of a 'new creation' has become, in many circles, the ONLY 'proper' and sufficient expectation of the supernatural. Many will say, the phenomenon of a transformed life has been evidence enough to draw millions to the Christian God and his son Jesus. True enough. For many, the supernatural has been relegated to the fringes of Christianity. Overt miracles are not necessary for salvation.

A transformed life is certainly a strong witness, but it is not enough to bring the kingdom. And, apparently, in God's eyes, this is not a legally sufficient testimony to end the age. The law requires *'two or three witnesses to establish a matter'*.

The Problem

The world has been given the witness of a transformed life. Hundreds of millions can give direct, personal, testimony to this power. But Christianity has fallen short in their witness in two areas—truth and power.

In spite of what Christianity may claim, to be the supreme guardian of truth, measuring for both an adequate witness without and within, we fall far short. This book, promoting a prophetic reformation, is full of specific examples, and there are many, many more. Christianity is far from unified in doctrine, and one faith. We have had truth enough for a gospel of salvation, but not enough for the gospel-of-the-kingdom.

The evidence is clear. Truth and power are related. Truth begets power. And Christianity today, cannot demonstrate with absolute power, the truth and intimacy with God it claims. The whole premise of our argument here is that when Christianity has adequate truth it will have adequate power. God can't trust a childhood church with adult power.

Power corrupts. Both natural power and supernatural power. We have to address both. The supernatural is powerful medicine, even dangerous. Understandably, it attracts attention. It can be used in the right way or the wrong way.

Segments of Christianity have even sworn off the supernatural. For them, proper miracles ceased after that first generation.

We have even learned that there can be something fleshly (wicked) about too much super-natural emphasis as Jesus reminds us:

> He answered, "A wicked and adulterous generation asks for a miraculous sign! But none will be given it except the sign of the prophet Jonah. (Matthew 12:39)

Unfortunately, because of our 'traditional salvation gospel', many, through lack of knowledge or faith, have lowered their expectations of the Body's identity and what we are called to do. Who are we? What are God's expectations of us and earth? Is there a role for us we have not expected?

Many see the gospel-of-the-kingdom testimony as the same testimony we have preached for centuries. With whatever degree of truth and power we have had, our testimony has been sufficient for the task of reaching a pagan world.

But there can be little doubt that Moses, Elijah, and Jesus operated in special dispensations of truth and power much different than we see today. Likewise, the coming gospel-of-the-kingdom testimony will be at a scale unprecedented in the church age and even human history.

A Super-Church?

If that is so, the question must be raised again, how will this happen? What will transform Christianity into a super-church able to bring this unprecedented testimony of truth and power to the whole world? Does the Bible give us an expectation and a formula for such a transformation? The answer is certainly, yes!

But, before it can be this testimony to the world, Christianity must choose adult truth. Part of that truth is the need to radically reorganize itself.

We will try to state this issue in generic terms first, hoping not to get bogged down in theological minutia at this time. Let's start with the big ideas, the prophetic ideas, the rest will come later. One should first try to gain a clear picture of the first principle.

The Power of Two

We must understand by now the nature of truth—it is binary. Like a coin, a single truth has two sides. They are different, and at times, appear to conflict with each other. It is interesting to note that the whole modern digital world runs on the concept of twos. Binary, '1's' and '0's', off and on. Very elementary on the surface, but oh so powerful. Even in technology, we can see how powerful this simple concept really is.

From the beginning of Biblical history, we see this unfolding principle of the twos. Heaven and earth, light and darkness, holy and common, male and female, power and authority, executive and legislative, law and grace, spirit and truth. The list goes on and on.

Successful human government (Biblical Israel, and U.S.) are designed with two authorities (King, priest or prophet; legislative and executive). This design tempers corruption and falsity. The founders of the US government understood this Biblical principle and designed government around it accordingly. They understood the danger of a single point of unchecked authority. They designed a national government around the concept of a separation-of-powers—a system that would mitigate the human tendency toward power abuse.

Jesus also, in forming the government of the church groomed 'the three' for leadership. Peter, James, and John were entrusted with top leadership. Peter and John represent the two foundations, Apostle and Prophet, with James as the Judge.

Jesus left the church in the good hands of the Holy Spirit. He didn't dictate formal government structure. The church had to experience its childhood on its way to adulthood. It didn't need all-truth and all-power during these last two millenniums.

As we have said repeatedly, adulthood would come later (in our day). It is a prophetic transition driven by the initiative of the 'sons'. Do we want all-truth and all-power? Do you? Are we able to keep the commandment to preach the gospel-of-the-kingdom? It can only happen if we bring a new power-managing order to Christianity.

> *For the kingdom of God is not a matter of talk but of power. (1Co 4:20)*

Do we see the validity of this principle of two so far? It's hard to deny. God divides to reveal specific truths or functions that are complimentary or inter-dependent of each other. Understanding both sides of the truth 'coin' and how they properly interact is our goal. And there are many 'coins'. Essentially resolving all of them is the heritage of Christianity, who is being led into all-truth.

Our greatest challenge at the moment is to understand ourselves, Christianity, and what must be done to comply with the demands of our imminent prophetic ministry.

Two Authorities

Today, the human institutions of Christianity are divided and contentious with each other. This is largely the result of the lack of a clear prophetic authority. To finish our ministry to this world, that must change. Bringing unity or oneness to the Body is just one of the challenges facing us. In this short discourse we can't hope to deal with all the internal issues facing Christianity, but we can point to the principle solution clearly given in Scripture. We won't discuss the formidable challenge of 'how' this can happen in any detail, other than to say it will come via supernatural prophetic power.

Rather we will just introduce the 'what' should happen here. There needs to be a longer and more diverse debate in the near future. Let the reader, and especially the leaders, examine their own hearts and positions concerning this subject.

The whole prophetic model proposed in this book hinges on this 'impossible' transformation of Christianity. It will happen. God's will on earth cannot be done apart from Christianity's prophetic reformation.

Today, all Christian authority flows from a singular Apostolic (Pastoral) leadership, whether it be a single person or council. We generally call these distinct authority networks denominations (and there are thousands of them). All denominational authority is contained within (or below) this singular top authority. We are not aware of a single denomination today that has, or even recognizes, a true TWO authority structure as defined Biblically.

Notice: 'God's household is'...

built on the foundation of the apostles and prophets...(Ephesians 2:20)

In God's sovereign work in the church, the last 2000 years, the multiplying of denominations has been permitted, perhaps even beneficial. However, this is not how the church must end. We can presume that this has come about largely because of the absence of a true prophetic authority. It has been a necessary childhood process.

But now we must realize the need for a corrective remedy—two separate and distinct authorities within the universal Body. Without implementing this advanced Biblical governance, Christianity will remain as it is, unable to fulfil it commanded commission.

Specifically, the two authorities are expressed within the functions or ministries of apostle and prophet. These terms are very familiar to

Christians, and there is great debate over how they work or even if they truly exist today. But briefly, and in the context of this discussion, let's examine their essential functions, and how they work?

As to nature or personality, one is a 'truth authority' (prophets or prophetic) and the other an 'executive authority' (apostles or pastoral). One is tuned to truth and the strategic plan of God—how it should be carried out; overseeing doctrine, and monitoring practice. The other is adept in outreach and community—interacting with people, discipleship, and needs ministry. These two authorities, the one dealing with the narrow path of truth, the other the broad path of the 'masses' have a natural tension between them.

In a submitted, ordained inter-relationship, the prophetic informs the pastoral in strategic issues, and maintains internal order. The pastoral is the primary voice of community within, and outreach to the external world. We can see how this arrangement, and only this arrangement counteracts the dangerous effects of power.

This separation-of-powers works in civil government (United States), in personal relationships (marriage), and in ecclesiastical government (the Church). We even see that this functional separation-of-powers submission derives from the Godhead. This beautiful self-governing and self-balancing relationship is based on willful submission rather than ambition, ego, or a struggle for power. It recognizes and honors the gifting God has placed within humble, servanthood humanity. This submitted authority mechanism counteracts the dangers of a single authority power structure over the long-term.

In principle, this governing order being pervasive in life, seems beautiful and rational. Who would argue against it? The unfortunate answer to that question could be, and has been throughout history—the 'ruling authority' (executive authority).

Having overwhelming influence, numbers, and resources, the ruling authority holds all the cards in their hand, except one—truth. The tension is truth verses expediency. In practice, the ruling authority is affirmed (at least initially) by the masses. They, the rulers, are uniquely adept at communicating to the masses (for good or evil) and likewise, the masses uniquely respond to this authority. This is how human society, both secular and sacred, is designed by God.

And generally, as the ruling authority goes, so go the people. (Or probably even more correct, as the people go, so goes their authority; people eventually get the leaders they deserve).

For our discussion here, 'ruling authority', is simply church authority. At the highest level, it is effectively an Apostolic authority. Every Christian denomination has one. This leadership defines doctrine, membership, and practice. But this single authority structure is prone to abuse.

Pastoral leadership is hollow without its connection to the people. Its very existence is to interact with people. The people bestow honor, recognition, and rewards on those whom they perceive are serving them (or the higher good). Therefore, it is a natural tendency that the ruling authority is highly sensitive to the state of the people. As the people trend in a certain direction the pastoral leadership will eventually flow with it, even while knowing better, and/or marginally resisting.

The spectacle of Arron responding to the masses and making a golden calf at Mount Sinai, is an example of the powerful influence of the people on leaders. What Paul is telling us here in Ephesians is that by design there are (should be) TWO autonomous authorities active within the larger body ministry. Had Moses been present in the example above, the golden calf incident would not have happened.

Any given body, whether it be a single church or a denomination, should be under the oversight of TWO authorities—a Prophetic authority and a Pastoral/Apostolic authority. While there should be mutual submission to the absolute principle, the inter-play between the two is pliant. There is room for diverse personality and function, but there needs to be a central authority. Notice this tribal design:

Every man of the children of Israel shall pitch by his own standard, with the ensign of their father's house: far off about the tabernacle of the congregation shall they pitch. (Numbers 2:2)

The pastoral authority is the executive leadership of that body; it manages day-to-day business; it effectively defines and maintains body (tribal) identity. This top leadership and its traditions define the character of the denomination. There is room for distinct tribal personalities.

The prophetic authority, on the other hand, deals with high-level principles and long-term prophetic strategy at a universal level.

While the pastoral authority is closely connected to the identity of its body, the prophetic authority, on the other hand, is more generic. Each deal with different aspects of spiritual administration—one is a truth ministry, and one is an executive ministry. The full spectrum of Messiah's ministry to earth is found within this binary, inter-related, priestly order. [And we must remember that there is yet another priestly order (Levitical), soon to be functioning (on earth) within this universal order.]

Yet a time is coming and has now come when the true worshipers will worship the Father in spirit and truth, for they are the kind of worshipers the Father seeks. (John 4:23)

Spirit and truth, heart and mind, male and female are foundational elements of human society. And for the Body of Messiah, this binary truth must also translate into distinct functions of government and authority as well.

The hierarchical system within each denomination or church often imitate an (apostle/prophet) system of checks-and-balances in directing decisions of theology and practice. But each denominational system is essentially self-contained, ultimately having a single point of authority. This cannot stand in lieu of a true two authority, separation-of-powers, structure. The essential idea behind an apostle/prophet separation-of-powers is that the 'prophet' is outside of any given denominational structure.

Imagine large denominations such as the Catholic Church, Baptists, Methodists, or Presbyterians submitting to a prophet not directly associated with their denomination; a prophet ordained to make judgements on theology and practice.

Thinking this through, one realizes that the whole Christian denominational structure is due for a radical transformation. Denominations were a necessary accommodation in an age without advanced prophetic authority. But, the coming of an authoritative 'truth ministry' will begin a transformative process within Christianity itself. One can begin to see the mechanism by which Jesus' prayer for 'oneness' might be realized.

As a whole, Christianity is NOT expecting this prophetic disruption. They are not expecting a credible Prophetic authority to appear in their midst, outside of Apostolic authority. In fact, there are major elements of Christianity that don't even believe the ministries of apostle or prophet are active today. However one might define the ministries of Apostle and Prophet, the church has been led, virtually exclusively, by some form of apostle/pastoral leadership up until today. The pastorals have brought us thus far, but…

The Days of 'Elijah'

One leg of Paul's apostle/prophet 'foundation' has been relatively dormant over these last 2000 years. Christianity has been running largely on 'spirit' This is typical of childhood. But the spirit ministries will never journey far enough into the wilderness of 'truth' to discover its fulness. They never want to journey far from 'immediate need' and 'engagement with people'.

That can only come via a truly independent prophetic authority. The truth is, Christianity as a whole does not have this essential apostle/prophet governing order today.

This is why, for all Christianity's success, it cannot go any further than it has. It cannot finish the prophetic journey; it cannot deliver on the adult gospel. The gospel-of-the-kingdom preached in apostolic times, with power, cannot be preached today. Christianity's 'house' is not properly wired. Connecting gospel-of-the-kingdom power (needed for today's testimony to all nations) to this house would likely burn it down.

But as the new popular song declares: 'These are the days of Elijah'. A new prophetic wind has begun to blow. Victory is assured. God has promised a glorified, unified, adult Body. Since the Reformation, 500 years ago, and especially over the last 100 years, major transformations have progressed. We are now ready for 'the end' (and the restoration that follows). The gospel-of-the-kingdom is a prophetic gospel. It can only be discovered by the prophetic ministry, and it can only be delivered by the apostolic (pastoral) ministry. [We will talk more about 'Elijah' in Chapter Eight: HOW IT ALL BEGINS—HUMAN INITIATIVE]

The Body will soon reform (or mature), write the script, and receive all-power. This can happen when it is righteously aligned and ordered internally. True leaders will respond to the Spirit and submit to ordained order. Prophetic Reformation is necessary to gain the understanding and trust necessary to implement this new prophetic order. Yes, the world will surely be conquered, can only be conquered, with prophetic truth and power.

Chapter Five

A NEW PROPHETIC GOSPEL

Preparing the Final Truth and Power Gospel

To review: We have the promise of all-truth. We have seen the work of the Holy Spirit quickening the pace of truth-seeking over the last 500 years. Looking ahead, we see the present challenge of defining and writing a detailed, legal, model or script describing the end-of-the-age period (Chapter 3: A NEW PROPHETIC MODEL). With transformed thinking, we have come to realize the need for an internal, separation-of-powers, re-ordering of the Body by integrating a truly independent and authoritative prophetic ministry.

The Gospel-of-the-Kingdom

We can now discuss the renewed gospel—the 'gospel-of-the-kingdom'. The decades long, end-of-the-age period, is initiated by a special 'testimony' given to the world called the 'gospel-of-the-kingdom'. Executing this vital 'testimony' is one of two prophetic commissions entrusted to an empowered church in Matthew 24. Here is the first commission:

And this gospel of the kingdom will be preached in the whole world as a testimony to all nations, and then the end will come. (Matthew 24:14)

We should stop and note two points: Who are the 'preachers' here, and is this a 'command'? As explained further in this book, WE are the preachers, and YES, it is a command given directly to us by Jesus.

This is not the gospel of salvation that has been preached for 2000 years and continuing today. So, what is it? The gospel-of-the-kingdom has many dimensions so it is hard to define in a few words, but let's attempt to extract its most essential nature:

The gospel-of-the-kingdom is a testimony of unprecedented clarity given to the world for the purpose of revealing, in supernatural terms, the one true God and his truth. A final testimony, fully entrusted to a human agency, spoken to the people of earth with unparalleled <u>truth</u> and <u>power</u> before 'the end' and an imposed 'new world order'.

We have to note the problem here. While Christianity has been able and willing to go the ends of the earth to share the good news of Jesus' saving faith successfully, today, it is absolutely incapable (even if it wanted) of preaching the gospel-of-the-kingdom to the world. The big hurtle is the phrase mentioned just above: a testimony spoken with UNPARALLELED TRUTH and POWER.

Fulfilling this unprecedented testimony, which will be followed by world repentance, can only be realized with a house put in order as we discussed in the previous chapter. A new prophetic presence (authority) must be accepted and integrated into the Body of Christ which today is overwhelmingly led and controlled by the pastoral ministry.

This is a 'physician heal thyself' reform necessary to perform the critical ministry of revealing God to the world before 'the end'. Conforming to these demands is our act of obedience preceding this glorious testimony. How can we speak to the world with authority when our house is clearly out of order? We have major disagreements, especially about truth and doctrine. We have fractured into thousands of denominations. Oneness is one of the adult promises and it is for the benefit of the world:

> *I in them and you in me. May they be brought to complete unity to let the world know that you sent me and have loved them even as you have loved me. (John 17:23)*

Oneness is required, as a testimony to the world. This gospel-of-the-kingdom is not typical evangelism, although preaching the gospel-of-the-kingdom will likely result in the greatest 'turn to God' repentance the world has ever seen. Evangelists, please take note! The greatest evangelistic outreach will begin with a prophetic reformation.

This gospel is a unique face to face encounter with the living God, with his people, and his truth, confirmed with massive demonstrations of the supernatural. For a brief moment the 'faith-curtain' will be pulled back for all to see reality as it truly is.

Jesus calls this new commission the 'gospel-of-the-kingdom' given to the world before 'the end'. This is a testimony similar to Elijah on Mt. Carmel, but on a worldwide scale. The world will be challenged in its false philosophies and religions: *"How long will you waver between two opinions?"* (I Kings 18:21). They will be shown the absolute reality of the God of Abraham, Isaac, and Jacob, and his son Jesus.

The 'gospel-of-the-kingdom' includes a forceful and painful confrontation with world powers. Following patterns from Torah, the end-of-the-age generation will begin with an Exodus, including the testimony of ten 'plagues', bringing the world to its knees. The old world will end and a new world will begin. The 'sons' will be revealed and begin a 'reset' of the world, its people and government systems. We have a remarkable picture of this 'conquest' and 'transformation' in Isaiah 40 and Micah 7. The end result is not a familiar Christian message, but *'the nations will turn to God'*. Here is the Micah Scripture, note the reference to the Exodus:

> *"As in the days when you came out of Egypt, I will show them my wonders." Nations will see and be ashamed, deprived of all their power. They will lay their hands on their mouths and their ears will become deaf. They will lick dust like a snake, like creatures that crawl on the ground. They will come trembling out of their dens; they will turn in fear to the Lord our God and will be afraid of you. (Micah 7:15-17)*

Christianity's pastoral ministry has been focused on the evangelization of the world, but the 'salvation and living' message alone cannot bring us to the Biblical kingdom revealed in the Bible. Only with a renewed prophetic gospel, the gospel-of-the-kingdom, implemented with force, will we complete our objective to see the world acknowledge the one true God. With this gospel of truth, the pastoral (apostolic) ministry will have access to unprecedented power to demonstrate the reality of the kingdom with healings, deliverance, and miracles.

Past Prototypes

In a real sense the end-of-the-age is a reboot of Adam in Eden. In the original story we are told this:

> *Then the man and his wife heard the sound of the LORD God as he was walking in the garden in the cool of the day...(Gen 3:8)*

Adam and Eve had a testimony, a (near) face to face encounter with God. As God remakes the likeness of Eden in today's world, he will give man a similar intimate encounter with himself. The gospel-of-the-kingdom is effectively this same very personal testimony. The world will know God was among them.

This veil-lifting type of testimony has been given to man on other occasions. Three notable similar testimonies were: in Egypt with

Moses; at Mt. Carmel with Elijah; and in the ministry of Jesus and the apostles.

The gospel-of-the-kingdom is a message with an unambiguous demonstration of power, proving the reality and the identity of the one true God. The message asks the world—how long will you deny your creator exists? How long will you embrace false religions and false philosophies? Note the three examples below:

At the time of the Exodus, Moses appeared in Egypt confronting Pharaoh's obstinance:

> ... or this time I will send the full force of my plagues against you and against your officials and your people, so you may know that there is no one like me in all the earth. ... But I have raised you [Pharaoh] up for this very purpose, that I might show you my power and that my name might be proclaimed in all the earth. (Exodus 9:14, 16)

Many centuries later, Elijah confronts his world on Mt. Carmel:

> "Now summon the people from all over Israel to meet me on Mount Carmel. And bring the four hundred and fifty prophets of Baal and the four hundred prophets of Asherah, who eat at Jezebel's table." (21) Elijah went before the people and said, "How long will you waver between two opinions? If the LORD is God, follow him; but if Baal is God, follow him." But the people said nothing. (1Kings 18:19 & 21)

And two thousand years ago, with Jesus and the apostles:

> Jesus went through all the towns and villages, teaching in their synagogues, preaching the good news of the kingdom and healing every disease and sickness. When he saw the crowds, he had compassion on them, because they were harassed and helpless, like sheep without a shepherd. (Matthew 9:35-36)

In principle, the 'gospel-of-the-kingdom' was preached, with power, to each of these generations, and judgement soon followed. Greater clarity requires greater accountability.

Adam walked with God in the garden. We can learn a valuable lesson from this insight. At that time, there was little room for creative philosophies that denied the existence of God or a created universe. Adam had no confusion, he knew God face to face, and yet he disobeyed.

Surprisingly, man's disobedience, even rebellion, against God has little to do with his direct knowledge of God. Many would say, or think, that an absolute knowledge of God would dictate one's compliance to God's demands. But we learn from Adam, and human history, that this is largely not true.

Knowing that God exists does not dictate our response to him. Responding to God and complying to his righteousness must come from something deep within, something we might call 'faith', (compliance to an inner directive) not from the absolute truth (of knowing God).

Nevertheless, it does seem right and necessary that God, at times, must reveal himself as God and creator of all things, and reveal an absolute standard of righteousness and grace. This has been God's pattern in human history. A testimony is witnessed; the record is written; but then, consistent with this age of faith (6000 years), God withdraws his overt presence.

Since the 'fall' and the birth of billions of people (with millions of ideas), mankind's confusion about God, his existence, and his righteousness, has greatly multiplied. Many grow up in environments, spiritually, scientifically and philosophically, denying the truth of a creator God, and his righteousness. The world must have one last 'testimony' before 'the end'.

Also, we should note the pattern of these special visitations in the formation of God's major institutions. The Moses testimony began the corporate institution of Israel. The Jesus testimony began the formal institution of the Church (Christianity). We see that great testimonies like this precede the initiation of God's (the universe's) foundational institutions. Human history now includes a mature Israel, and we have a mature Christianity, each have a 'childhood prominence' of roughly 2000 years. But there is yet one spiritual institution to be formally initiated (governmentally) on this earth—the kingdom. It too, following a clear pattern from history, will have its special testimony as well.

The gospel-of-the-imminent-kingdom is God's gracious answer to intentional and even unintentional confusion about God's existence and his purposes for mankind. Once again, God will give mankind direct, unimpeachable, knowledge of himself and his righteousness as the final institution, the kingdom, is inaugurated worldwide. In a real sense, the gospel-of-the-kingdom is the final message of this kind.

Section Two
THE PROPHETIC STORY OF MANKIND
From Genesis to the Second Coming

Remember the former things, those of long ago; I am God, and there is no other; I am God, and there is none like me. I make known the end from the beginning, from ancient times, what is still to come. I say: My purpose will stand, and I will do all that I please. (Isaiah 46:9,10)

I will surely bless you and make your descendants as numerous as the stars in the sky and as the sand on the seashore. Your descendants will take possession of the cities of their enemies, and through your offspring all nations on earth will be blessed, because you have obeyed me." (Genesis 22:17,18)

And this gospel of the kingdom will be preached in the whole world as a testimony to all nations, and then the end will come. (Matthew 24:14)

Chapter Six

DISCOVERING 'THE END' IN OUR FIRST RESPONSIBILITY

We all lead busy lives! Let me count my commitments for today... However, in contrast to the wonderful, yet consuming story of my life, we have the prophetic story of mankind. That larger story is the subject of this discussion. To help escape the hypnotic trance of life, we must set aside the immediate cares of today and take a brief loop back to the beginning.

God created man in his image. This is no trivial responsibility for mankind. Being made in the Father's image, it is reasonable to conclude that the sons were given the responsibility to manage all of creation. We are not simply God's favorite pet going along for the ride, rather, his intention was that we would have full standing (inheritance) in the divine family and, therefore, full responsibility.

For man, understanding and reengaging in this original responsibility SHOULD BE the primal driving force of prophecy. Prophecy, as has become popular in the modern church, is typically driven by identifying spectacular events. But events are secondary to the character transformations they are designed to affect. And those critical character transformations are far more indicative of the prophetic 'times and seasons' than all the fireworks of the mainstream news cycle.

Essentially, to understand prophecy we must participate in prophecy. And foremost in that process is to understand the renewal required of those called to lead. Character transformation, such as renewing the mind (thinking truthfully) and mastering sin are key prophetic goals of the end-of-the-age.

But how will God create God-like men? Can God program mankind to understand faith and mercy, victory and loss, compassion and forgiveness, good and evil? God is not creating a fantasyland with robotic mannequins. Many qualities such as faithfulness cannot be programmed into man: they must be experienced; yes, they must be earned. Somehow these qualities needed to be instilled via a process beyond an instantaneous creation. In that first creation, Adam was created fully grown. There would seem to be a message in that. Mankind needed a childhood!

Childhood Found

In Adam's fall, God took the opportunity to give mankind a childhood. Somehow, within God's perfect universe, he would make room for planned disobedience and rebellion. This was necessary for God to give us a childhood that would include failure, suffering, and even death. Through this process, man would have a new awareness instilled deep within his spirit. He would gain a first-hand understanding of the disaster of disobedience and rebellion, and, just as important, the victory of overcoming. Man would learn to manage and control the beautiful, as well as the dangerous qualities and appetites of being human. He would embrace responsibilities greater than self. He would learn to understand suffering and ultimately to overcome sin, demonic forces, and the appetites of self.

Adam bypassed childhood. But he, his garden, and his walk with God, gave us a taste of the ultimate goal and intentions of God. But it wasn't to last. Paradise was lost, not to God's surprise. Because of their sin, Adam and Eve would leave their freely given paradise, and enter a painful world of struggle, disappointment, and death.

Not having human management as intended, God, as parent, would step in as the interim manager. And just as any human parent would do, God measured out corrective punishment or discipline. He cursed or afflicted various aspects of creation for the duration of the discipline. Effectively, God 'troubled' man's domain. The man would now work by the sweat of his brow, the woman would have pain in childbirth, and creation would groan in unrest. There would be conflict and chaos. Humans would not be allowed to sustain life by eating of the tree of life, thereby experiencing the fruit of sin – death.

*"Do not mortals have **hard service** on earth? Are not their days like those of hired laborers?" (Job 7:1)*

Hard Service – Searching for the End

This is the new stream in which all life will swim! But was this meant to last forever? No, not forever. Then how long? To discover this truth is part of man's new challenge. When should the punishment; the curse; the **hard service**; end? And how? This is the foundational challenge that good prophecy must address and ultimately answer.

Defining the Right Goal

The goal is critical. For many today, their goal is heaven. But this goal confuses the reward with the responsibility. Isn't this man's tendency—to focus on benefits rather than duty? The wrongly perceived goal will lead to a faulty impression of the journey. Such is the case of today's Christian prophecy.

Man's **hard service** came as a result of a failed responsibility. That responsibility has not been rescinded; it has, however, been out of reach. Returning to our first responsibility, not heaven, should be our top priority?

Jesus reminded us of this first responsibility with his striking words:

> *"But seek first the kingdom of God, and his righteousness; and all these things shall be added unto you." (Matthew 6:33)*

The complexity of this command is not so easy to understand. A child initially perceives the adult world as a fantasy, even what little he knows about it. And any command perceived as a fantasy, is a command misperceived.

The two commissions in Matthew 24 have been misperceived because we have not been thinking as adults (prophetic grownups). Looking back, who would have imagined a prophetic program that called for Moses to conquer mighty Egypt, and slaves to defeat giants in the Promised Land? *"The land is good, but we are not able!"* Yes, we underestimate who we are (an identity crisis); therefore, we misperceive what we have been called to do.

To clarify Jesus' sense of our prophetic capabilities, re-read the Upper Room Discourse (John 14-17), Jesus' last sermon, a Passover sermon. It is not a sermon motivating us on the joys of heaven. Rather, it is a sermon on identity promises while here on earth as we grow into the likeness of the Son. Take note of the many 'character destinations' promised therein—I like to call them the 'kingdom alls'. As you read this sermon, look for the following:

- All Peace
- All Truth
- All Power
- All Joy
- All Glory
- All Love
- All Strategy
- All Oneness

- All Holiness
- All Separation
- All Reconciliation

Jesus describes a 'Body of Christ' that our current teachers will tell us cannot exist on this side of heaven. But truth and transformation IS the first goal of prophecy, not the rapture, the Antichrist, or the tribulation, the current nucleus of Christian prophecy.

The core of true prophecy is the truth of our responsibility and the internal transformations we are prophetically promised – while still flesh and blood humans.

What that responsibility means in today's prophetic context is not an easy read, but it is what we must understand and embrace. What does God require of us, and when will our **hard service** end? The end of **hard service** and the reengagement of mankind's original responsibility are closely related. These are the radical prophetic truths we must come to understand.

By now, these words from Jesus' model prayer should be burning in your mind:

> *"your kingdom come, your will be done on earth as it is in heaven." (Matthew 6:10)*

Now, read those words again, and ponder their meaning. Close your eyes and meditate on the magnitude of what Jesus is saying.

Then consider these ideas: Do you perceive these radical prophetic truths as a personal responsibility, or are they just a sacred hope? What are your expectations? Are you thinking as a child, or as an adult? Is your frame of reference that 'someone else' will do it? Or, are you expecting to be personally involved in the victorious testimony to the whole world... before the Second Coming, as displayed in the Upper Room Discourse?

Do you now, at least, recognize how the subtle distinctions in your thinking could affect your prophetic expectations? We may have presumed that the 'big stuff' would be handled by God. But the dilemma is that the 'big stuff' is the adult stuff. And the big stuff is precisely the adult responsibility we have dropped and must now take up once again.

One might imagine a very appropriate response from a good father. He might say, *"When you are wise enough to understand and return to that responsibility, I will begin to release you from your **hard service**. Your **hard service** will end when you are finally prepared to be my partners again in managing my business."*

Learning the Business

But what does it mean 'to be my partners again'? Is it a question of blind obedience, or of being faithful to follow all the rules, or obeying Scripture? Is this what God wants from us? Is that what love is all about—obeying all the rules? Well, in a way yes, but…

True love is fulfilling the <u>secret</u> desires of the beloved. It is knowing someone well enough that you can respond to their deepest, unspoken desires. This sounds like personal romance talk and it is, but it also translates to our relationship with God and our perspective on prophecy.

We are taught to obey God. For fundamentalists, we are taught that the Scriptures are the literal words of God, and, 'If God said it, I believe it'—no questions asked. But, unfortunately, the unspoken opposite of that is: 'If it's not written down in Scripture, I will not believe it (or do it)'.

Simply doing what we are told in the Bible, isn't too far off for Sunday School, but as we grow up, life is not quite so simple. Obedience is more than just submissive compliance to commands on paper.

A deeper understanding of obedience is defined by the example of King David's actions and God's response. David's impulse to build the Temple is the classic Biblical example of positive human initiative.

Initiative which must be consistent with the heart and purposes of God, of course.

Briefly, God had told Israel, in great detail, to build the Tabernacle in the wilderness. Many, many chapters are spent emphatically describing every detail of the Tabernacle. Its design is commanded in virtually every detail.

The presence of God and the entire priesthood were centered on this Tabernacle. Four hundred years later, after the conquest of Canaan, the remains of the Tabernacle were standing in Shiloh. By now David had brought just one piece, the Ark of the Covenant, to Jerusalem and it was sheltered by a tent. Up until then, David's life was dedicated to defeating Israel's enemies, and building his own palaces.

But as those immediate demands were fulfilled, something shocking happened. David had a thought that was seemingly contrary to Scripture. He would build a permanent Temple of wood and stone here in Jerusalem.

But God had not told him to do this! He had not told any of Israel's leaders to do this. "Restore the Tabernacle God gave us in the wilderness, David", the Bible scholars of David's day would have advised, driven by their knowledge of written Scripture.

But David had sensed the heart of God. He had discerned the unspoken will of his Sovereign Lord. This act would initiate the dimensions of Israel that we know today. A new dispensation would begin. Promises unforeseen would now flow from the grace of God.

With this Temple, Jerusalem would forever bear the name of God; the people of Israel would have a home safe from their enemies. And beyond that, inspired by this thought, God himself would build an eternal house for David and a heritage, which would eventually beget the Messiah (See 2 Samuel 7).

Can we formulate a principle based on this example? Yes. God often works in two phases. He instructs man with the temporary or the partial, but establishes the permanent with man's response and initiative. Let me state this again so you don't miss the magnitude of what I am relating. God instructs man with the temporary or the partial, but establishes the permanent with man's response and initiative.

If we translate this idea prophetically, we'll see that the world and the garden God gave to Adam was only intended to be a prophetic illustration, but not the eternal reality. It was not the fullness of God's plan. Adam himself was not yet finished.

The fall of man started a new journey. That journey would include **hard service** and a time for man to grow in the wisdom and the knowledge and the mercies of God.

We now know God and his ways. He has given us the Prophets, the Priesthood, the Scriptures, the Messiah, and the Holy Spirit to travel with us. In spite of man's terrible failures, God has shown us a way of forgiveness and restoration. And…

> *'According as his divine power hath given unto us all things that [pertain] unto life and godliness.' (2 Peter 1:3 KJV)*

And therefore, there would come a time when men would respond like King David, and build a (permanent) world that God had envisioned from the beginning. God will not dictate the time and the details like he did the Tabernacle, instead, like David and the Temple, God would speak through an inner discernment, motivated by man's own love of God and knowledge of his purposes.

David is a model of how the kingdom must come. Our Father is inviting, indeed waiting, for his sons to build his kingdom. We pray, *"Not our kingdom, but thy Kingdom come…"*

How will the Kingdom Sprout?

Yes, mankind's initiative is paramount in the process, but can we be more specific. Will the manifested kingdom on earth sprout in the U.N., the Catholic Church, Judaism, or in the Southern Baptists? Will it sprout from within a major organization? Will it spring out of earthly power and institutions? This is all highly unlikely for explainable reasons. So then, how will the kingdom manifest?

When it is time, it will spring forth from the smallest seed; from a mustard seed—from the prophetic. Great institutions will not foresee the pathway to the kingdom. Even Jesus' true body, Christianity, will initially reject the kingdom, not understanding it for what it is. Instead, it will start with the smallest seed—'the prophet'. Perhaps its beginning will even be a single 'seed' within the prophetic ministry of Messiah.

"...The kingdom of heaven is like to a grain of mustard seed... Which indeed is the least of all seeds: 'but when it is grown, it is the greatest among herbs, and becometh a tree...'" (Matthew 13:31-32 KJV)

Man was given a dream, paradise in the Garden, and the responsibility to manage it. He stumbled! Yet our God is a God of second chances. He has given us (mankind) a 'second dream'.

But this time there is a key significant difference. The second chance requires man to struggle to define and implement it. It will come from his own impulses, consistent with learned truth and the will of God. To be certain we are serious this time, mankind must first discover exactly what that responsibility entails and why. It's not just an employee-type responsibility; it's an ownership-type responsibility—sonship.

But to affect an external kingdom on earth, it will require an internal transformation. A new order discussed in "Section 1: PROPHETIC REFORMATION" (specifically: "Chapter 4: A NEW PROPETIC ORDER").

As Jesus frames it, our destination must be character transformation: Christ-likeness (Ephesians 4:13); all-truth (John 16:13), etc. We were foreigners to God, but through Jesus we have become 'family', because...

'...a servant does not know his master's business.' (John 15:15)

There is a catch however; God has NOT fully revealed the 'second dream'. It is not written down specifically in so many details. Yet, this is the beauty of God's ways, his mysteries. He leaves room for man's expression. As part of man's responsibility, he must contribute to the final shape of the kingdom. Wow!

Building the Kingdom, like David's Temple, must be driven by man's response. In Matthew 25 Jesus gave us the parable of the Talents. In it, the master gives each of three servants a different number of talents, and then he leaves on a long trip. When he returns, the servants are expected to have multiplied those resources, indicating their commitment to the master's business.

What are the 'talents' in Jesus' prophetic sermon? Study will show that they are the prophetic 'secrets of the kingdom'. The servants were expected to multiply 'secrets' on their own. God walks with us for a way, but then he leaves us to listen and be attentive to the still small voice of the Spirit within (1 Kings 19:12). As wise managers, we must translate the principles and patterns of God into the complex world in which we live. We have the written Word, but...

> 'When the Spirit of truth comes, he will guide you into all truth.'
> (John 16:13)

Let me introduce you to an important prophetic concept. This may stretch your prophetic muscles. The Bible is ALL TRUE, but it is not All-TRUTH. In other words, everything written in the Bible is true, however that does not mean that the Bible contains every truth that God intends for us to know. He leaves room for discovery via our relationship with the Spirit. It is the Spirit who 'guides us into all-truth'!

The End in the Beginning

God is expecting a super-human effort in our search for truth. We must turn to the Book of Genesis to anchor our prophetic search. There we see the original nature of man. He is made in the image of God and his responsibility is to take 'dominion'. We see a family in a life-sustaining garden living off the bounty of the earth. And then of course, we see the 'fall' and God's response to it.

This contrast between the original paradise on earth, and the current state of **hard service** should be our first concern. It should be evident we have not come to 'rest' in the fullness of God's goodness. This is the nature of the prophetic dilemma we have inherited. Our responsibility is to seek out a remedy. We can be certain that we have all the 'clues' (or the talents) needed to resolve this mystery. Truth is the first hurdle; the truth will set us free.

As we continue through the Scriptures, we learn the nature of God and his overarching purposes for this journey we are on. We begin to see that all things work together for good. We start to recognize the 'fall' as a time of 'childhood', which ultimately proves to be a positive development for mankind. The general timing of our prophetic mandate, regarding the 'end-times', can be stated in terms of two markers, or prophetic signposts, which find their roots in the first few chapters of Genesis. Let's consider each...

Marker One - Nearing Adulthood

The 'fall' has given mankind a childhood of preparation and struggle. However, we have been given all the 'talents' that we need to outgrow it. In God's good world, childhood should not be forever. It would seem that our childhood and our **hard service** will end when a remnant of mankind, those led by the Spirit, are ready to become adults.

"Ready to become adults"? That idea might sound familiar to many people. Yes, this rite of passage is recognized in Judaism as a Bar Mitzvah, "a young son becomes a member of the adult world, which comes with rights and responsibilities". It signifies a son who has become a man.

Could this be what human history, from Adam to our current day, is waiting for? Is all of creation waiting for mankind's childhood to end and his adult world to begin? Paul clearly points to that reality in Romans 8 when he says:

> *"The creation waits in eager expectation for the sons of God to be revealed." (Romans 8:19)*

The 'sons to be revealed'? For Paul, an orthodox Jew, this would most certainly be related to a son's rite of passage. The term "bar mitzvah", in the sense it is now used, cannot be clearly traced earlier than the 14th century. Instead, Paul would have likely used a generic description of this rite such as 'the revealing of sons', rather than the modern term 'Bar Mitzvah'.

This is a profound statement by Paul. Reading the full statement, we see it clearly points back to Genesis and the 'curse'. Paul continues...

> *"For the creation was subjected to frustration, not by its own choice, but by the will of the one who subjected it, in hope that the creation itself will be liberated from its bondage to decay and brought into the glorious freedom of the children of God. We know that the whole creation has been groaning as in the pains of childbirth right up to the present time." (Romans 8:20-22)*

Paul is affirming that the universe is having a childhood and **hard service** until 'the sons' become men.

When a son becomes Bar Mitzvah'd, ideally, he is now mature enough to have legal access to the resources of the father. Jesus also pointed to this reality, this access to 'everything', in his Passover Discourse (Upper Room Discourse, John 14-17):

> *"I no longer call you servants (children), because a servant does not know his master's business. Instead, I have called you friends*

(adults), for everything that I learned from my Father I have made known to you." (John 15:15)

So, the end of the **hard service** comes when God once again has faithful partners who are ready to take on management responsibility, to take on 'the master's business'. This is a spiritual maturity. This has come through a complex process of multiple dispensations over human history. Some will choose to follow the cloud of God's provision and duty, others will not. The faithful will grow and mature as spiritual mankind. All the 'troubling', negative events of human history should not distract us from seeing the quiet, slow, but steady growth of the sons of God.

Marker Two – Nearing Sabbath

So, nearing spiritual maturity (Bar Mitzvah) is one prophetic indicator marking the end. Do we also see any other obvious markers in the beginning of Genesis that would indicate the nature and timing of the end of **hard service**?

Yes, God gives us the pattern of Sabbath. By watching his example in creating, we begin to learn God's ways and see how fundamental the Sabbath pattern is to everything he does.

By the seventh day God had finished the work he had been doing; so on the seventh day he rested from all his work. (Genesis 2:2)

As God's revelation unfolds in history, we discover the importance of time. In the structure of the week, a 'day' may have prophetic or symbolic definitions, such as 'a day equals a thousand years' (Ps 90:4, 2 Pet 3:8). Therefore, a prophetic week could be considered seven thousand years.

And just as God 'worked' six days, man's 'laboring by the sweat of his brow' can be associated with a 'work day' activity. Man must

'work' (in sin) for six days, or six thousand years; but in God's
economy 'laboring' ends on Sabbath. This pattern would likely indicate
God's intention to end man's **hard service** at the end of the (prophetic)
work-week and the beginning of Sabbath rest, the Millennium. This is
all part of building a prophetic model.

Nearing the End

So, we now have two markers, drawn from patterns in Genesis, of
how and when the end (of **hard service**) will come. We have a spiritual
maturity (the sons reaching the stage of adulthood), and a chronological
completeness (the end of the work-week and entering 'rest'). Notice
how the basis for our prophecy framework is coming from Genesis, not
from Revelation.

Jesus appeared, '*in the fullness of time*' (Galatians 4:4), at the
beginning of the fifth prophetic day—Thursday. His Body has had
2000 years of childhood growth with testing and lessons via the work
of the Holy Spirit. Chronologically, that puts today's current world
right in the transition from the six-day 'work-week' into the Sabbath
Millennium.

Many other signs indicate we now live in a prophetically climactic
time of history. The coming of truth has benefited humanity, both
spiritually and materially. Human advances in science, industry, and
politics were led and undergirded by spiritual advances. The
Renaissance, the Scientific Revolution, and the Industrial Revolution
were some highpoints in the human journey.

It can be argued that the diverse advancements in the welfare of
mankind is largely a product of the gospel. And along with those
advances came the possibilities of greater peace and prosperity. Peace
and freedom, necessary qualities for true prosperity, is a product of the
personal self-government that flows from peace with God and his
commandments.

Friday Morning

Starting Friday morning, prophetically (1517), what we now call the Protestant Reformation burst forth in western civilization. Like new 'prophetic hormones', greater truth, as promised, would begin to flow in the human bloodstream. The common man would now have cheap and direct access to Scripture and spiritual revelation. The Holy Spirit began a new work in various 'bodies' and 'sectors' to prepare them for their participation in a final restoration.

As we mentioned in Chapter 1 spiritual reformation gave rise to revivals, nations, revolutions, and movements, chief among them America and Israel. A new prophetic world-order is slowly emerging.

Today's Christian church began as a legitimate sect of Judaism, with the founding fathers all Torah keeping Jews (Israelites). Since then, Christianity has very forcefully severed itself, both theologically and literally from its parental body. This severing was prophetically necessary, but it was theologically flawed.

Because of this, prophecy has suffered as well. Christian prophecy has become New Testament (Revelation) centric, rather than Torah centric. We will not be able to finish our journey without becoming reconciled with our original Hebraic theology and prophecy.

This is essential to understand the secrets of the kingdom and adult prophecy (all-truth). The spiritual maturity and the chronological moment has, or will soon, reach completion. What does this mean? And what should we expect?

Finally – the End?

Over 6000 years, much has changed. God had revealed himself through Israel, the Torah of Moses, and the prophets...

"...but in these last (two) days (2000 years) he has spoken to us by his Son." (Hebrews 1:1-2).

Not only 'spoken', but the eternal Word has become flesh and dwelt among us! In fact, in Adam's failure and Jesus' provision, mankind would find even greater identity and perfection. Man would become like God having knowledge of good and evil. He would GROW in wisdom and the knowledge of God.

And even as the Son came to earth and became a man, God is setting-apart a remnant on earth and giving them power to literally become sons of God, members of his divine family in heaven.

The Son brought us the realization of the 'kingdom of heaven' and he gave us power to become part of that privileged calling. Those who call on the Son become part of the Son, in an intimate marital relationship. This is where the prophetic story of mankind is today.

Sundown – the Return?

The sun is setting Friday night (the end of the sixth millennium); humanity has had a week of hard service; and it is time for the Messiah to come (return) and set up the kingdom!

Not so fast! Generally, that is what both Christianity and Judaism believe, although with great variations. Ultimately, yes, the Messiah will come and formally claim his kingdom. But what has been missed, especially by Christianity, is the PRECURSOR to the formal kingdom. The prophetic Sabbath begins with a period the Bible calls 'preparing the way'. Essentially, a time of spiritual harvest and formation. It must come first.

The Precursor – Preparing the Way

This lengthy precursor period and the events in it can generally be referred to as the end-of-the-age, or sometimes the end-of-the-world (the world as we know it). This period will likely be decades long for reasons we will discuss further.

The return of the Messiah takes place at the end of this period. And he will come to a newly birthed kingdom of welcoming subjects. He will begin the formal rule of the kingdom that has already been initiated by his disciples during the precursor period. This precursor period begins the Millennium which many properly see as a 'day' of 1000 years.

We have now reached the relevant mother-lode of end-time prophecy. How we understand this precursor period before Messiah returns, will determine our understanding of God, his program, and how we and our loved ones will respond and contribute in these critical days.

Thus far, we have discovered that to end the world's **hard service** we need 'adult *Adams'*, who will come forth at the end of the prophetic 'work-week'. These mature believers make up a unique prophetic ministry capable of properly managing God's end-of-the-age business.

Chapter Seven

MORE PROPHETIC VOCABULARY

In the prophetic insights to the end-of-the-age in the previous chapter, the two markers were drawn from the first chapters of Genesis. This is an important principle of prophetic truth; 'God reveals the end at the beginning.'

> *"Remember the former things of old: for I [am] God, and [there is] none else; [I am] God, and [there is] none like me, <u>Declaring the end from the beginning</u>, and from ancient times [the things] that are not [yet] done, saying, My counsel shall stand, and I will do all my pleasure." (Isaiah 46:9-10 KJV)*

Only God can do this—to his glory, and only the sons of God will fully understand—to their glory. God wrote future prophecy into mankind's past history. The future is spoken to us in a vocabulary created from the events of the past. Jesus utilizes this principle in his Matthew 24-25 discourse. As we noted earlier, he uses activity from the past, the Exodus and Joseph in particular, to reveal the prophetic future.

End-of-the-age prophecy has resisted deciphering because this principle of taking our prophetic vocabulary from the past has not been understood and applied adequately. From Jesus' own mouth, we now recognize two commissions based on events from the past.

In Chapter 1 we defined the terms 'end-of-the-age', 'restoration', 'prophetic model', and 'Millennium commissions'. Now we need to take a moment to identify and relate a few more terms.

In our study we have discovered two 'talents' (secrets of the kingdom), literally, Exodus and Joseph. And as Jesus revealed in the Talent Parable (Matthew 25), the master would give us two secrets, go away, and if we 'invest' those secrets well, we will discover more secrets, etc. Secrets beget secrets.

To be valid (complete), a prophecy model must have a Biblical framework. A Biblical framework is a mega-pattern into which all smaller events or patterns are placed. We make the challenge in this book that there are no popular Christian prophecy models that have a Biblical framework. Without a framework, the Scriptures and pieces of your prophecy model, are speculative and arbitrary.

The Holy Grail of end-of-the-age prophecy, which is largely missing from today's Christian prophecy, is to find a framework that contains the entire end-of-the-age. It's like finding the 'picture' that comes on the front of the end-of-the-age 'puzzle box'. Does one exist? Yes!

The End-of-the-Age Framework Found – The Journey

Our prophecy model is based on the two Millennium commissions. They are the patterns of the Exodus, and the fourteen-year Joseph ministry.

We know the Exodus is the beginning of a journey Israel took to the Promised Land. We also have a pattern of a special generation in the wilderness, but how does Joseph's fourteen-year pattern fit into the journey story? This is a very interesting study which we will just briefly highlight here.

First, the Joseph commission is seen in the pattern of the Joshua ministry – conquering and dividing the Promised Land. Notice the instructions God gave to Israel earlier:

> *When you have <u>entered the land</u> the Lord your God is giving you as an inheritance and have <u>taken possession of it</u> and <u>settled in it</u>, take some of the firstfruits of all that you produce from the soil of the land the Lord your God is giving you and put them in a basket. Then go to the place the Lord your God will choose as a dwelling for his Name...(Deuteronomy 26:1-2)*

Restated: "When you enter the land (take possession and settle) bring the firstfruits." When do you bring the firstfruits? The Jewish Sages take commands like this very seriously and precisely. Thankfully for us they have, answering the question of how the Joseph ministry is part of the journey.

In this case its best just to quote a Jewish commentary from Rabbi Abraham Stone, THE JEWISH PRESS – Friday, August 26, 1994, (Page 16) (our underlining):

Complete Conquest of Israel

When the Israelites conquered Cannan the first time, in the days of Joshua, <u>it took 14 years to make this conquest complete</u>. A study of this historical event is also linked with some relevant halachic rulings in Jewish life. Thus, in the opening verse of Parashas Ki Tavo ("When you will enter"), we read:

> *"And when you will enter the land which Hashem gives you for an inheritance and you have conquered it and you dwell in it" (Devarim 26: 1); Rashi comments: This teaches us that <u>they were not obligated to bring Bikurim (first-ripened fruits to the Beit Hamikdash) until after they had conquered and divided the entire Land</u>. This rule, of a completed entry, is applicable not only in our parasha, where the Torah specifies, "And you have*

> conquered it and dwell in it" [Deu. 26:1] but, as our Sages teach
> (Kiddushin 37b): Wherever the Torah uses the term "when you
> will enter" (concerning the observance of a mitzva) it means
> after conquering and dividing the entire Land.
>
> Conquering and dividing the land is not an individual action.
> After each person receives his territorial share in Israel he still
> does not bring bikurim. This mitzva began only after the 14 years
> in which the Jews conquered and divided the entire Land of Israel
> amongst the tribes (Zevachim 118b).

Other Jewish sources say the fourteen years were divided seven and seven. Seven years to conquer, and seven years to divide. How beautiful are God's designs! In Chapter 2: Cosmic Identity, we discussed how Christianity sees the Promised Land as heaven. We can see how that would frustrate a true prophetic model. Jesus' second commission points to Joseph and the conquest of the Promised Land. This is the critical conclusion of the end-of-the-age. We will discuss what this Joseph ministry is, and why it is so vital to the kingdom, in other documents.

So, we see that God has woven these two discrete events (Exodus and Joseph) into a grand-narrative, also taken from the pages of scripture. We will refer to it as the **Journey**. It is a story written in human history and recorded for our prophetic benefit. It is history as prophecy. Who can compare to our God!

Adding a generation in-between the two commissions, and we have a story we are all familiar with – the journey from Egypt into the Promised Land. We will explain this much more in other parts of this book and in future books.

So, there is an Old Testament account that gives us a larger, 'picture' framework of the entire end-of-the-age. An Exodus, a wilderness generation, and the formal possession of the 'Promised Land'. This 55-year journey from Israel's Biblical past is also a prophetic rehearsal of a similar **Journey** the whole world must make at the end-of-the-age (also likely 50+ years). Very briefly we calculate 55 years as:

- 1 year - Moses returned to Egypt and confronted Pharaoh leading to the Exodus
- 40 years - in the wilderness
- 14 years - Joshua conquers and divides Canaan (Joseph)

The reality that God would use this **Journey** story as a framework for all end-of-the-age events should not be surprising. This **Journey** is God's mega-pattern for all life. He has, and will, continue to use this pattern over and over again.

We are reminded that the journey itself was expressed within an even more fundamental pattern of God–the Moedim, the appointed-times of the Lord, commonly called the Feasts of the Lord. This sacred yearly cycle reveals special times to meet with the Lord. With them, we commemorate events of the past and rehearse events of the future. They walk the community of God through a complete spiritual 'life-cycle' each year. Again, everything God does is associated directly or indirectly with his appointed-times.

Remember, both Israel and Christianity were formally established by the first Feast–Passover. Jesus was crucified even as the lambs of Passover were being slaughtered, at that very hour. He was buried in the grave on the second Feast, Unleavened Bread; and he rose again (three complete days later) on the Feast of Firstfruits. Fifty days after Firstfruits, as defined by Torah, Christianity had its Pentecost, just as the Jews were observing Shavuot (the Feast of Weeks) in the Temple, commemorating the first offering of the Torah 1500 years earlier. Notice the beautiful symmetry–the giving of the Law and the giving of the Spirit at the same appointed-time.

Death, burial, resurrection, and empowering with the Holy Spirit, the repetitive pattern is undeniable. Christianity was formally "incorporated," duplicating the same prophetic steps as Israel. The two spiritual bodies are indelibly related, yet intrinsically distinct.

A key to comprehending end-of-the-age prophecy is understanding these two spiritual entities and how they are related within a third entity, the Kingdom. Natural Israel, Christianity, and the Kingdom integrate (not assimilate) into a working whole, mature and functioning in their respective roles. All three have, or will make, the same **Journey**, starting with an Exodus.

Jesus uses the Exodus, Joseph, and 'this generation' as discrete building blocks for an end-of-the-age **Journey** pattern. With two of God's major institutions, Israel and Christianity, following this **Journey** pattern (and Feast pattern) as history, how can anyone doubt that soon the next institution, the Kingdom, will be formally initiated on earth following this same pattern of the **Journey**?

But this is a much, much different end-of-the-age than Christianity is currently expecting. Today, there are no popular Christian prophetic models that include Jesus' commissions. They do not even include Passover, thinking Passover has already been 'fulfilled'. Why have we failed to incorporate these beautiful and prophetically strategic patterns from our past into our current prophetic models?

This also, is a complex question. We'll explain in greater detail this **Journey** pattern in future books, but one concept is clear. Christian prophecy is largely Revelation (the Book of Revelation) centric rather than Torah (Genesis, Exodus, etc.) centric. It creates a prophetic model built around the final, short, but spectacular events of Revelation. In it, mankind and demonic forces are largely caught up in a whirlwind of provocation, survival, and judgement. This is not a good picture of Adamic responsibility, and it is not generally based upon the prophetic vocabulary of the past. Current prophecy is informational (spectators observing events) not transformational as intended. Again, when we read Jesus' Upper Room Discourse (John 14-17), we see a far different view of Jesus' noble expectations of humanity.

Being able to explain these mysteries to the world and what they mean as the events unfold is the destiny of the prophetic priesthood. Prophecy is what drives world events; they are not arbitrary.

We have a choice. One can be ignorant, supportive, or as this document will stress, active agents, in the greatest events of earth's history. But Jesus warned that the cares of life, the immediate, could blind one to the prophetic jet-stream that drives human existence.

Humans are not tumble weeds to be blown about by the winds of life. No, we are called first to transform our own thinking, to understand reality, and then implement a kingdom based on truth. Prophecy is our reality-check. Are we spectators, or are we players in this drama of life? We may have forgotten our nobility; if so, here is a reminder:

> *Lift up your heads, O you gates; be lifted up, you ancient doors, that the King of glory may come in. (Ps. 24:7)*

An adaptation of Psalms 24:7 and Romans 8:22:

> *"Through you, O gates of mankind, the King of glory will come, Open wide, you ancient doors, that creation may be free."*

Yes, indeed, God is looking for just such a noble people. It is astounding that God should call us 'gates', and 'ancient doors'. As 'doors', those 'revealed', will become the resting place of the King, and his eternal expression!

So, we have identified 'the **Journey**' as the overall framework of the end-of-the-age, but that will need translating into more concrete terms and events for today's world which we will do as we continue below.

The Bible is not meant to be a scholarly work. Its narrative style can be at times very general and at other times extremely precise. Add to that the burden of translation into different cultures and languages and even versions within the same language. Through all of this, students and scholars attempt to interpret, systematize, and apply, the truths of Scripture.

Add to this, human personality, vocation, motivation, and intention, and we have an almost insurmountable challenge. One can see why there are thousands of Christian denominations and perhaps hundreds of serious prophetic models as 'truth' candidates. But prophecy is the answer to all this turmoil.

Getting to the Bottom Line - Restoration

Patterns are a major part of God's spiritual vocabulary. Jesus' ministry, as the Lamb of God, is largely explained to us by Old Testament patterns. A prophecy model that has patterns within patterns should have great validity.

The function or purpose of the **Journey** is *Restoration*. Jesus revealed two commissions, the Millennium commissions, as the defining events of the **Journey** framework. But what is their function taken as a whole? They are intended to initiate the kingdom and prepare the people of earth for his literal return. This is the assignment he left with his followers before he left.

Those apostles named themselves after that assignment. The term 'Christian' was assigned by outsiders later, but the early messianic (church) believers named themselves, 'The Way', as in, 'those who are preparing **the way**'. Therefore, the function of the **Journey** is to 'prepare the way', or effect *Restoration*. This term represents a period of time that may be 50+ years long, that we also call the 'first generation' of the Millennium.

'Restore' and 'restore all things' are a Biblical term that harkens back to the Garden of Eden with its image of a perfect paradise. By using the Garden paradise and sinlessness as a backdrop, it is easier to properly relate to the word 'restore'.

Prophetic *Restoration* is not just a general revival or repentance, or personal revival. Its scope is universal, we are directed back to a future where our **hard service** will end.

Now, in one sense we can never go back to that paradise and the innocence that mankind had before eating of the tree of the Knowledge of Good and Evil. Our world is now much more complex and diverse, but God has not abandoned the goal of paradise. He has a plan to restore the 'goodness' of this universe and bless humanity.

So, the purpose of the end-of-the-age and the **Journey** is *Restoration*. This *Restoration* implies removing at least a portion of the universal 'curse', the **hard service**, caused by Adam, and resetting today's human society consistent with the ideals and laws of the eternal kingdom.

Our primal model for this *Restoration* is Israel's journey from Egypt into the Promised Land. To direct that journey there were two key leaders, Moses and Joshua, and two key campaigns. Moses was the wilderness prophet, and Joshua lead the campaign to settle the Promised Land. These two campaigns directly relate to the two commissions of Matthew 24.

Notice that Israel's King (David) did not bring the people out of Egypt, nor did he conquer the Promised Land initially. These two *Restoration* ministries are distinct from the 'King' ministry [Most of Christianity sees the King as the restorer, which is incorrect]. *Restoration* must come first, to prepare Israel (and the world), for their King.

Today's world is symbolically the equivalent of the Biblical 'Egypt'. The *Restoration* soon to come, is the start of what could be called the first generation, of the Millennium. Typologically, the Exodus is the beginning of the Millennium. *Restoration* runs from the coming of a prophet, 'Moses/Elijah' in Egypt, to full entry into the 'Promised Land'. These are two distinct human initiatives lead by members of Jesus' body. One thing should be clear, Messiah does not come 'to prepare the way' for Messiah; his people do.

Complex, new ideas can be difficult and confusing at first until a new vocabulary has been developed and disseminated to an interested community. It gives the learning and dialog process a common foundation. To that end, we have attempted to formulate terms that can and will be used in our subsequent discussions.

So, to summarize these terms relationally, we could say: end-of-the-age prophecy is framed by a Biblical framework we'll call the **Journey**. Its purpose is to effect *Restoration*, by two major commissions (Millennium commissions) which are assigned to the **first generation** of the Millennium. One can see how resolving the two commissions of Matthew 24, opens the door to the only systematic prophecy model that can accommodate ALL prophetic pieces.

Restoration – Telling the Story

Establishing the kingdom and the will of God on earth today is an extremely complex and somewhat lengthy operation. Up to this point we have presented the *Restoration* in mostly conceptual terms. The *Restoration* is the beginning of the adult world. To finish our story here, we'll add some flesh to this cosmic event in three areas.

Chapter 8: How it all begins - Human initiative
Chapter 9: Building a born-again world
Chapters 10-13: Missing the obvious—Three people groups

Chapter Eight

HOW IT ALL BEGINS—HUMAN INITIATIVE

But as many as received him, to them gave he power to become the sons of God, even to them that believe on his name: (John 1:12 KJV)

I tell you the truth, anyone who has faith in me will do what I have been doing. He will do even greater things than these, because I am going to the Father. (John 14:12)

The driving force of the *Restoration* must be human initiative, positive, Spirit directed, human initiative. Much of today's Christian prophecy focuses on a figure called the Antichrist. While it is a Biblical idea, it is not the focus of Biblical prophecy and it should not be our focus. The Antichrist is an 'anti' force which arises in reaction against some final 'positive' force. That positive force is the *Restoration* driven by the sons of God. Our energies should be directed toward understanding OUR BUSINESS of the *Restoration*. Without knowing that, we will never understand evil and the anti-forces.

Good Citizenship

The *Restoration* is a program directed by man to bring 'good citizenship' to earth. Obviously, this raises a number of questions. The two foremost – who is 'man', and what is 'good citizenship'? And a third would quickly become, 'how could this be done'?

What is good citizenship? We purposely use this word as a generic (non-religious) word for the more Biblical term righteousness. Righteousness carries the baggage of sectarian 'doctrine' which can get unnecessarily contentious today. So, in its most basic form, this book is not about sectarian issues, it is about good citizenship.

By citizenship, we ultimately mean how individuals, families, communities, and nations interact with each other and with God. This is what kingdom and righteousness boil down to. As Jesus summarized the Law:

> *He answered: " 'Love the Lord your God with all your heart and with all your soul and with all your strength and with all your mind' ; and, 'Love your neighbor as yourself.' " (Luke 10:27)*

Of course, as this book reveals, there are some cosmic (prophetic) issues as well, but those complexities end where the Old Testament ends. Here is the last verse:

> *He will turn the hearts of the fathers to their children, and the hearts of the children to their fathers; (Malachi 4:6)*

Bringing order and harmony between God, government, and family is good citizenship. This is what we are after. From human civilization as it is today, how do we get to a culture of good citizenship? What are the rights, privileges, and duties of a good citizen of earth?

Human Government

How do we bring world government into this place of good citizenship, of peace? Jesus wept over Israel, as its leaders knew not the way of peace.

> *As he approached Jerusalem and saw the city, he wept over it and said, "If you, even you, had only known on this day what would bring you peace--but now it is hidden from your eyes. (Luke 19:41,42)*

The way of peace. Do we (the earth) know the way of peace? After 6000 years of human civilization; with extensive diversity of culture, government, language, habitat and experiences, do we know what makes for a good citizen? After 200 years of the industrial revolution, technical revolution, worldwide travel, the explosion, accumulation, and dissemination of information on every subject, has man come to some conclusion about how to live?

What is a family? What is an education? Who is God? Were we created? It is literally stupefying to realize mankind still cannot answer these most basic questions. What is male and female? Is life in the womb a baby? What does it take to raise an innocent, new-born baby for him NOT, just sixteen years later, to terrorize, plunder, rape, and steal at every opportunity?

Check the statistics: divorce, addiction, violence, sexual licentiousness, institutional corruption, persecution, and disease, the world is not at peace.

Would it be reasonable to say, we've had enough time? We should have got it by now? Mankind should have come to some 'ideal' conclusion by now.

Has there been any progress? Well, yes. Man is thinking. Occasionally, there are breakthroughs and advances. Man has this curious nature that wants to take dominion. In our opinion this is a God-given sentiment. Instinctively, man wants to manage, or fix society. Of course, any 'fix' can be well-intentioned or vilely self-serving.

The Bible gives us a history of human society – advances and setbacks. Particularly interesting is the formation of nations and languages (we will talk more about this in the next chapter). This record was given to us through the story of Israel. On Mt. Sinai Israel was given the principles and instructions of their covenant (or constitution) we call Torah.

Through this covenant of love, mankind now had the renewed hope of paradise. Given Torah, Israel would now begin to codify a system of law that defined perfection, personal and national. Fifteen hundred years later God sent his only begotten Son, born of a woman, born under this law, to this earth.

Messiah, Jesus, was the perfect expression of the Mosaic law. And while he was a member of the divine family, he was not perfect because of his divinity. We are told he set that privilege aside; he emptied himself of his deity (Philippians 2:7). He was perfect because he was a perfect expression of the Mosaic law as generally defined by man.

It had taken four thousand years to get to this point. Mankind, In the form of Israel, now had a system of national and personal law that could express, what God considers, perfection. This was confirmed by God, in the fulness of time, in the unique life of Jesus. But how this law and this life will impact the world will take some surprising turns.

Unfortunately, mankind was not yet ready for such perfection. Even Israel stumbled. Their religious center, the Temple, was destroyed. The job of bringing that perfection to the rest of the world would now pass to another 'nation' (Christianity). They would translate the principles of Jewish Law into the foundations of Western Civilization. It would take time and be less than perfect, but through the transformation provided by the cross, and at times the sword, the pagan world would be conquered.

Many 'messiahs' would come with different messages. The empires of Greece and Rome would facilitate the translation of a 'Jewish' religion (and Bible) into, what we now call, a 'Western' dialect. We would see the formation of a distinct 'Gentilized' church, its eventual split into two sects, Eastern Orthodox and Roman Catholic, and then into the numerous denominations we have today.

A new 'Abrahamic' religion / political system, Islam, would start and expand into the region with military conquests. Sometime later, we would see the Dark Ages, followed by a new humanistic Renaissance.

In recent history, the last one hundred and fifty years, new theories of government and political ideologies would address perceived faults. They would build new social orders eliminating, what they saw as the 'negative influences' of religion, private property, capitalism, and class exploitation. Those 'isms' such as Marxism, Communism, Socialism, Anarchism would promote various types of 'revolutions', violent or otherwise.

The struggle for truth, and an 'ideal human society' was costly. But the fundamental ideas of justice, equality, and compassion would slowly take root. Revolution, defiance, schism, and reformation, bred any number of new philosophies and creeds even into the twenty-first century.

We now have a catalog of religious and political systems. A well-developed library of 'isms', written and tried. Along the way we have inherited many Charters, Constitutions, and Declarations of Rights. The new, building upon the past. They are man's attempt to build a 'just' legal code for mankind. Let's trace that thread through the last 1000 years – the legal high points that have played an important role in civilizing the world:

Charters, Constitutions, and Declarations

(Mostly edited from Wikipedia)

1215: The Magna Carta (or Great Charter,) was effectively the first written constitution in European history. It established for the first time the principle that everybody, including the king, was subject to the law and guarantees the rights of individuals, including the right to justice and a fair trial.

1517: The Reformation, specifically referred to as the Protestant Reformation, was a schism in Western Christianity initiated by Martin Luther and continued by John Calvin, Huldrych Zwingli, and other early Protestant Reformers in 16th-century Europe. It is usually considered to have started with the publication of the Ninety-five Theses by Martin Luther in 1517 and lasted until the end of the Thirty Years' War with the Peace of Westphalia in 1648. The Peace of Westphalia was a series of peace treaties signed between May and October 1648 in the Westphalian cities of Münster and Osnabrück, effectively ending the European wars of religion. [The Thirty Years' War (1618–1648) and Eighty Years' War (1568–1648)] The Peace of Westphalia established a new system of political order in central Europe based upon the concept of sovereign states, which became known as Westphalian sovereignty. As European influence spread across the globe, these Westphalian principles became central to international law and to the prevailing world-order.

1620: The Mayflower Compact was the first governing document of Plymouth Colony.

IN THE NAME OF GOD, AMEN. We, whose names are underwritten, the Loyal Subjects of our dread Sovereign Lord King James, by the Grace of God, of Great Britain, France, and Ireland, King, Defender of the Faith, &c. Having undertaken for the Glory of God, and Advancement of the Christian Faith, and the Honour of our King and Country, a Voyage to plant the first Colony in the northern Parts of Virginia; Do by these Presents, solemnly and mutually, in the Presence of God and one another, covenant and combine ourselves together into a civil Body Politick, for our better Ordering and Preservation, and Furtherance of the Ends aforesaid:

1776: The United States Declaration of Independence is the statement adopted by the Second Continental Congress in Philadelphia on July 4, 1776. The Declaration announced that the thirteen American colonies at war with the Kingdom of Great Britain would now regard themselves as thirteen independent sovereign states no longer under British rule. With the Declaration, these states formed a new nation – the United States of America. Here is the Introduction and the first sentence of the Preamble:

> *When in the Course of human events, it becomes necessary for one people to dissolve the political bands which have connected them with another, and to assume among the powers of the earth, the separate and equal station to which the Laws of Nature and of Nature's God entitle them, a decent respect to the opinions of mankind requires that they should declare the causes which impel them to the separation.*
>
> *We hold these truths to be self-evident, that all men are created equal, that they are endowed by their Creator with certain unalienable Rights, that among these are Life, Liberty and the pursuit of Happiness.*

1787-1789: The United States Constitution (including the ten Bill of Rights) is the supreme law of the United States. The Constitution, originally comprising seven articles, delineates the national frame of government. Its first three articles establish the doctrine of the separation of powers, whereby the federal government is divided into three branches. Since the Constitution came into force in 1789, it has been amended 27 times.

1789: The Declaration of the Rights of Man and of the Citizen, a product of the French Revolution, was a major statement on man and society. These seventeen Articles written by General Lafayette with input from Thomas Jefferson, expressed the core 'citizen' values of the French Revolution. These universal 'citizens' rights here were generally only granted to male landowners.

1948: Universal Declaration of Human Rights (UDHR) consists of 30 articles affirming an individual's rights which, although not legally binding in themselves, have been elaborated in subsequent international treaties, economic transfers, regional human rights instruments, national constitutions, and other laws. The Declaration was the first step in the process of formulating the International Bill of Human Rights, which was completed in 1966, and came into force in 1976, after a sufficient number of countries had ratified them.

1976: International Bill of Human Rights was the name given to UN General Assembly Resolution 217 (III) and two international treaties established by the United Nations. It consists of the Universal Declaration of Human Rights (adopted in 1948), the International Covenant on Civil and Political Rights (ICCPR, 1966) with its two Optional Protocols and the International Covenant on Economic, Social and Cultural Rights (ICESCR, 1966).

Some legal scholars have argued that because countries have constantly invoked the Declaration for more than 50 years, it has become binding as a part of customary international law. However, in the United States, the Supreme Court in Sosa v. Alvarez-Machain (2004), concluded that the Declaration "does not of its own force impose obligations as a matter of international law."

Moving Forward

Where do we go from here? God has given man a season to ponder, test, and experiment. We now have a Tree of the 'Knowledge of Good', and the 'Knowledge of Evil', richly baring fruit. In God's mercy, and the will of our fore-parents (Adam and Eve), we have inherited a choice. It is time to grow up.

After 6000 years the empirical evidence is abundant. If we could call a world council and have an honest broker lay out the evidence, it would be clear. It would be clear to those with a pure heart and clean hands. Given an ideal deliberation, mankind COULD set the world in order, create a just, equitable, and compassionate world.

The problem is not firstly a problem of resources, knowledge and ability. It is a problem of the heart, the willingness to do what it takes. It is a problem of sin and a self-centered heart. This truth should be evident now.

So evident that we will not spend any more time elaborating the journey so far. Instead, we will move on to explain the solution. We will explain the process and the components that will bring righteousness, peace, and joy to the world. The 'how to' given to us by the Creator of us all.

So far, in this book we have traced the sacred and the secular journey of mankind to this place. Through our philosophers and our prophets, we can agree with this truth:

His divine power has given us everything we need for life and godliness through our knowledge of him who called us by his own glory and goodness. (2 Peter 1:3)

A Quick Review

Let's do a quick review of our discussions so far: We are moving from a childhood world to an adult world. We are moving from a work-week to a Sabbath. With the coming of truth, we can now 'think (or speak) like God' and create (recreate) a new world speaking God's vocabulary (patterns). In the mature Body of Messiah, we have adult leadership that can be an 'honest broker' (prophet) to the world and lead us through the required process. And finally, we have the legal precedents of worldwide Charters and Constitutions as models for a new charter that will soon be given to mankind, the Freedom Charter.

The tender leaves of summer are now appearing!

The Freedom Charter

The legal framework of the end-of-the-age is centered on two charters. They correspond to the two commissions of Jesus in Mathew 24 (v14 & v45). The first charter is the Freedom (or Exodus) Charter given to those who have 'come out of Egypt'. The second charter which is connected to the 'Joseph ministry' will not be discussed in any detail in this book. It comes decades later and is not a priority today.

Prophetically, the earth today can be seen as 'Egypt'. Egypt is where life begins and grows in childhood. We are 'born' or 'begin' life in Egypt, but the patterns of spiritual life show we must be 'born-again'; we must leave Egypt.

This process can also be seen, as we have noted, as moving from a childhood world to an adult world. Many things change in the new world. The Bible frames many of these changes in the mode of a charter.

A charter is a written grant by a sovereign power, by which an institution such as a company, college, or city is created and its rights and privileges defined. In our case the sovereign is God, and the institution is the 'adult world' (or 'Promised Land') we have been talking about. Let's spend a few moments dissecting the charter we are calling the Freedom Charter. (Since it is closely associated with the kingdom 'Exodus' it could alternatively be called the Exodus Charter)

It should be recognized that this whole process is complex and detailed. Our intention in this book is not to be the last word or the most complete word, but to frame these issues as clear as possible as a first reading with the expectation of continuing dialog.

We will use just the two key Scriptures below to formulate the particulars of this charter.

"Comfort, comfort my people, says your God. Speak tenderly to Jerusalem, and proclaim to her that her hard service has been completed, that her sin has been paid for, that she has received from the Lord's hand double for all her sins. A voice of one

calling: "In the desert prepare the way for the Lord; make straight in the wilderness a highway for our God. Every valley shall be raised up, every mountain and hill made low; the rough ground shall become level, the rugged places a plain. And the glory of the Lord will be revealed, and all mankind together will see it. For the mouth of the Lord has spoken." (Isaiah 40:1-5)

And...

The scroll of the prophet Isaiah was handed to him. Unrolling it, he found the place where it is written: "The Spirit of the Lord is on me, because he has anointed me to preach good news to the poor. He has sent me to proclaim freedom for the prisoners and recovery of sight for the blind, to release the oppressed, to proclaim the year of the Lord's favor." (Luke 4:17-19 & Isa 61:1-2)

If we break apart the specific clauses from the two passages above and combine them, we would create a single set of clauses something like the following:

1. That her (mankind's) hard service has been completed
2. Prepare the way for the Lord
3. Make straight in the wilderness a highway for our God
4. Every valley shall be raised up
5. Every mountain and hill made low
6. The rough ground shall become level
7. The rugged places a plain
8. The glory of the Lord will be revealed
9. Preach good news to the poor
10. Proclaim freedom for the prisoners
11. Recovery of sight for the blind
12. Bind up the brokenhearted
13. Proclaim the acceptable year of the LORD
14. Proclaim the day of vengeance of our God

15. Comfort all that mourn

The scope of this list of declarations is both personal and cosmic. Now, let's briefly describe some of these clauses by number:

#1 The Curse

#1 is speaking of the Adamic 'curse' (**hard service**). In particular it seems to indicate the Adamic predisposition to sin, sometimes called 'original sin' will be lifted. This is critical because it prepares the way for true human 'freedom', the end of sinning (conformity to the Son). We see the cosmic scope of this 'freedom' clearly in Paul's companion verses in Romans 8:

> *"The creation itself will be liberated from its bondage to decay and brought into the glorious freedom of the children of God."* *(Romans 8:20-21)*

#3-7 Class Inequity

#'s 3 thru 7 are dealing with another worldwide issue, class inequity. Most of the legal charters and 'isms' make class inequity and injustice a priority issue. Marxism, Communism, and some Socialisms identify class and its components, capitalism, private property, private ownership of production, as the source of social evil. These 'isms' contend that when government doesn't prohibit these social structures, they result in the exploitation of wage laborers, and a whole host of other 'oppressions' by the ruling class.

There is inequality in the world and the Freedom Charter will address it correctly and realistically. False humanism solutions such as Marxism and Socialism only make inequality and injustice much worse.

#9-12 The Lowly

#'s 9 thru 12 is addressing the lowly, the oppressed, the physical or psychologically impaired, and the misfortunate. This would also include prisoners (criminals), and the unruly. This is a big basket of people with very diverse situations leading to their lowly-ness. Some manage to share beauty and love even in, perhaps even because of their lowly-ness, some are defiant and rebels. There is nothing intrinsically virtuous in being poor or unvirtuous in being rich. One's bank account does not indicate righteousness, whether it be high or low. In one sense we are all lowly, and we are all called to lowly in heart.

False 'isms' like Marxism, use social standing as evidence of righteousness, the 'upper class' are oppressors, the 'lower class' the oppressed. This is a false measure. Only the kingdom will truly lift the lowly.

The New World

We see in these particulars the need of a new world. God, through the prophets, has identified for us what he sees as deficiencies in the childhood world, and what needs to be done to correct those deficiencies. The new world must make a radical break from the old. It is strong medicine, but it is necessary.

One's place in the new world is not necessarily based upon past achievements or lack of achievements in 'Egypt'. #4 & 5 show human status from the old world will likely change. This is truly a moment of grace. All are valued equally, none are ignored.

For just a moment, the normative principles of the kingdom will be suspended. Principles such as 'To those who have more will be given' and 'What you sow so shall you reap' will be set aside temporarily in this season of grace. These principles will be especially true as we continue, but here it must be different. In building a new world, we must start afresh, we must error on the side of grace. If you were lowly you will likely be increased, if you were high, you will likely be lowered (in the naturalistic sense).

Knowing the goodness of God, we can be sure this will lead to a better day for everyone. To see all mankind, high and low, enter a future of righteousness, peace and joy should enrich everyone. By starting fresh in a new 'garden', with justice and liberty for all, everyone will prosper in the long term. Think of the creative possibilities; think of a world where the positive energies of mankind are freed directed justly to the benefit of all. Imagine what is ahead of us.

These are the spiritual realities soon to come; the kingdom to come. No one is excluded. The lowly in heart will applaud this new hope. However, we can be certain that not everyone will want to take this journey as a good citizen. Pharaoh was not inclined to listen to Moses. It is unlikely the 'mountains' of this world will care for this idea of 'coming out of Egypt', of starting afresh. The 'mountains' are quite comfortable and safe in their neighborhood, 'childhood Egypt'. Most 'high' individuals and institutions will certainly resist any change of this nature.

So, we know how this journey must begin. The 'Pharaohs' of the world will need a special 'testimony', and they will get one. It took ten plagues to coerce Pharaoh to 'let the people go'. This is the 'testimony to all nations' Jesus spoke of. When it is over, everyone will see the power of the God of Israel, firsthand. Many will sign-on for the Journey, others will cling to a dying Egypt.

The Freedom Charter is the driving force behind this gospel-of-the-kingdom, the testimony to all nations before the end, as Jesus said in Matthew 24:14. That message must take many forms, shaped for a wide spectrum of 'authorities' on earth. But at its heart, it's a message we've heard before, 'repent, for the kingdom of God is at hand'.

A Suggested Charter

If we translate the elements discussed in the list above, together with other Biblical elements that need to be added, we might create a suggested Freedom Charter with the following twelve articles:

Article 1:   Repent, seek the Lord your God

Article 2:   I will free you and take you out of 'Egypt'

Article 3:   I will forgive your sins

Article 4:   I will heal and deliver you

Article 5:   I will remove your oppressors

Article 6:   I will set the captive free

Article 7:   I will restore your families

Article 8:   I will give you a perpetual inheritance

Article 9:   I will bless you

Article 10:   You must love the Lord your God and learn his ways

Article 11:   You must love your neighbor as yourself

Article 12:   But, if you forget, and turn away, I will smite the earth with a curse. (Malachi 4:6)

Remember, that this is a 'Reset' charter. It creates a level playing field from which a righteous kingdom can proceed. Through the 'testimony' and the 'reset', God will reveal himself to the whole world as he did with Adam when he walked with him in the garden. All false gods and false philosophies will be exposed.

The kingdom is not a totalitarian government. Once the 'Reset' is complete, the world will be given great freedom to grow, to create new institutions, and cultures, hopefully consistent with truth.

This is a test. As the world continues, people will find room to express their truest desires. If they fail to seek the Lord with all their heart, evil will blossom once again bringing tribulation and judgement on the land. Like a bottle of wine, after the shaking stops, the dregs will once again settle to the bottom and unfortunately the good wine will have to be separated once again (the antichrist judgement).

How the elements of this Charter are introduced to the world is a story we will tell in more detail in "Chapter 9: BUILDING A BORN-AGAIN WORLD (The End of the World)".

Elijah

To bring this transformation about, it will require prophetic leadership. As we said earlier, the end-of-the-age is only possible because (a remnant of) mankind has finally reached a certain level of maturity, willing and able to take on a new level of responsibility in managing this earth. Back in Chapter 3: A NEW PROPHETIC MODEL, we spoke about a metaphorical corporate adult *Adam* who would once again take on the responsibility of our forefather Adam.

The two components of *Adam* are the apostolic (pastoral) and the prophetic authority. Together, they provide a government administration of truth and power. But specifically, it is the coming of *Elijah* which is the spark of the end-of-the-age. *Elijah* is the prophetic authority and the guiding force of the transition to an adult world.

The Gospel-of-the-Kingdom

The renewal of this *Elijah* ministry is essential to fulfill the first commission commanded by Jesus in Matthew 24:14, (and also by Paul in Romans 8:19). This first commission is an Exodus type testimony revealing to the whole world in indisputable terms, the one true God, the God of Abraham, Isaac, and Jacob, and the Father of Jesus the Messiah.

This gospel-of-the-kingdom will be a complex message, delivered with absolute power, which would cover at least these three areas:

1)   Truth – Who is God, and his prophetic program

2)   Righteousness – The kingdom has come to earth; repent, become a good citizen

3)   Identity – The 'revealing' of the sons, then, in the wilderness, 'prepare the way of the Lord' (perfecting of the three people groups)

The gospel-of-the-kingdom offers a new legal charter of freedom, equality and peace, and identity. God will pour out his grace, but the powers of earth must humble themselves. The world must 'come out of Egypt' and willingly accept a new world-order.

Peace on Earth, Good Will to Men

The underlying message of the gospel-of-the-kingdom is peace; peace on earth, good will to men. The message would be delivered by a host of kingdom evangelists, under the guidance of '*Elijah'*, to both individuals and power institutions of all kinds, including Christianity.

It will be a traumatic time, designed not so much as judgement of evil, but as judgement of falsity. Judgement is coming to a world (particularly the Christian world) that can't discern truth, a world that wavers between opinions. And, judgement begins at the house of God.

Undoubtedly there will be resistance from world powers. Likely, the message will be received no better than Pharaoh's reception of Moses' message in the Exodus story. The messages will be backed up with both positive and negative demonstrations of power worldwide, such as healings, deliverance, and plagues. With increasing forcefulness, a testimony is given.

The kingdom must come! The kingdom and its righteousness; the will of God must be manifested on earth. Righteousness will come graciously, incrementally, and voluntarily, when possible.

Everything of Spiritual Significance Begins with Passover

As we said earlier, the kingdom begins with an Exodus. The prophet's closing message to the world is essentially this:

'The kingdom on earth will begin with Passover. The world must have a Passover, you must keep the Passover'

Yes, the next Passover; a literal Passover!

I am the LORD your God, who brought you out of Egypt to be your God. I am the LORD your God.' "(Numbers 15:41 NIV)

Who is God? Israel forever resolved that issue in the Exodus. Now, the whole world must resolve that issue. The world must know that the God of Israel is THEIR God as well. Eternally, the world will remember, the God who 'brought us out of Egypt'.

Man needs a reference point. If there is to be a Paradise (the Promised Land), there needs to be a place before Paradise—an Egypt.

The phrase 'out of Egypt' is used as a reference point over 140 times in the Scriptures, including this strange account:

> *When he arose, he took the young child [Jesus] and his mother by night, and departed into Egypt: And was there until the death of Herod: that it might be fulfilled which was spoken of the Lord by the prophet, saying, Out of Egypt have I called my son. (Matthew 2:14-15 KJV)*

Even the Son of God needed to fulfill the principle of 'coming out of Egypt' (an Exodus) spoken by the prophet.

Passover Again?

Our 'literal Passover' message will be staggering to some, but remember two things. First, this is not the first time God has required a literal Passover in the world outside of Israel. Passover did not begin in Israel; it began in Egypt. He first required it of Egypt, the (pagan) world of its day.

And second, everything of spiritual significance begins with Passover. In God's world, something is 'born' (or birthed) in Egypt, and then it is 'born-again'. This is the Passover pattern. The progressive advancement of God's will on earth (the kingdom) started with Abraham. As it advances into progressively larger spheres, each needs an 'Egypt' and a 'Passover/Exodus'. As we said earlier, Israel needed one, Christianity needed one, and now to bring the 'will of God' to the entire earth, the kingdom also will need a 'Passover/Exodus'.

Israel has not forgotten. For faithful Judaism today, a Passover sacrifice on the Temple mount has the highest priority. Orthodox leaders in Israel are now rehearsing such an event each year. The altar and the priests are ready. No Temple is needed for the reinstatement of this sacrifice. Each year now, faithful Judaism petitions the government of Israel to permit such an event. They are restrained from performing a Passover sacrifice by their government, concerned by the Arab and secular world's response.

Am I referring to a literal Passover sacrifice in the twenty first century? This is pure lunacy or worse to the world and, unfortunately, even to Christian world. It would not be lunacy to Jesus, Peter, James, John and Paul. There is absolutely no evidence that the early Jerusalem church, directed by the apostles, which functioned for many decades after the death and resurrection of Jesus, discontinued their participation in the Jewish Passover sacrifice. There is no theological basis for the end of the Temple system, the Priesthood, or the sacrificial system.

One can see the obvious disconnect between the modern, go to heaven Christianity, and the early apostolic church. This literal kingdom is a kingdom very few Christians are expecting.

Just Asking - How would you do it?

Let's interrupt our discussion for a moment and think about the issue here. How would you (or anyone) compel earth's seven plus billion people to do God's will? Really, specifically, if you had the platform and the power, what would you tell the world? Is God's will simply a spiritual confession, a clear choice, or must there be changes in behavior, changes in law, culture, etc.? And once a program is clearly mandated, how do you think the world would respond?

If you object to this plan of a literal Passover as the institutional beginning of the worldwide kingdom, which is built on 'institution building' patterns from the past, you must offer an alternative. Is there a single book, a website, or speaker that can explain God's will AND how it will realistically be imposed on earth—friend and foe alike? I'm not simply asking about kingdom concepts. I am asking how, realistically, will those kingdom concepts be literally realized throughout the earth.

Suppose you and your group (church / denomination) were responsible for an area 100 miles in diameter in some geographic area. How would you impose, or request, or plead with, the million people or so in your domain to do the will of God? What kind of government would you impose; what social changes would you decree and enforce (or attempt to enforce)? And once done, how likely is it that you and yours would agree with the million or so other (church) administrations around the world who must do the same in their community?

This is what it means when we pray...

Thy kingdom come, thy will be done, on earth as it is in heaven.

It must affect billions of people on earth. It's no wonder Christian prophecy focuses on the antichrist. As a villain, he's an easy sell. Our leaders can lift him up as THE obstacle to a God filled world, and, at the right time, Jesus and the angels will come and destroy the rebels.

Or, perhaps he will come and affirm all sincere efforts. Then, magically, virtually overnight, everything will change and fall into place. This is largely a fantasy.

In the hope that Jesus would do our job, the sons of God have diminished their adult responsibility. Relating to God as children, they have not resolved the Biblical pattern of the *Restoration*.

But there is no alternative to the *Restoration*. God will raise up a prophetic ministry which speaks with grace and power to the whole world. The message will be measured but forceful.

Today, there is no plan offered by the Christian world to bring this about. But there is a divine strategy to accomplish this transition. The only strategy that comes straight out of the first books of the Bible. And it's not a private journey freshly proscribed by some prophet, but a familiar journey, a journey traveled before. It is a story well-known by a large percentage of the world—a journey like past journeys, in sync with the ways of God. The sons are simply following in their Father's footsteps.

Judaism

Judaism is ready for their first Passover sacrifice, but 'Ishmael' won't let them. This is prophetically strategic.

There would be a certain prophetic beauty if '*Elijah's*' first kingdom Passover would correspond to the first Levitical Passover sacrifice on the Temple Mount in Jerusalem in nearly 2000 years.

If it was up to Judaism it would have already happened. But they are not called to enforce the kingdom on the whole world. However, they do feel compelled to reestablish proper Judaism as soon as they are able.

If left to today's Islam, it will never happen. Nevertheless, this sacrifice will mark the beginning of the Millennium kingdom. It would seem that the Christian *Elijah* is the missing piece of this great prophetic drama.

It seems quite likely that *Elijah* would orchestrate such a beautiful scenario. After clear supernatural evidence he is speaking for God, all three Abrahamic faiths will cooperate in this first act of the kingdom. Regardless of anyone's objections, including misplaced Christian theology, the world must keep a literal Passover. Presumably, the literal event would stay consistent with the pattern; all males must be circumcised, lambs slain, and blood applied to the doorpost, just as it was done in the first Exodus.

This is the first kingdom act required of the world. A measured, doable, first step in the coming of the kingdom to the whole earth. This is not about the judgement of evil directly; it is about a clear testimony and simple obedience and compliance to the prophet's voice. Christians, Jews, Muslims, Hindus, atheists, pagans, and any others not named above, must comply or defy the command.

A Prophet Like Me...

This prophetic Passover, and an all-powerful *Elijah*, is a shocking notion for most Christians and it will require much more study and debate at another time, but here are two passages from both Deuteronomy and Acts referring to *Elijah* 'the prophet' and showing the need for obedience to his command. From Deuteronomy:

> *The Lord your God will raise up for you a prophet like me from among your own brothers. You must listen to him. ... If anyone does not listen to my words that the prophet speaks in my name, I myself will call him to account. (Deuteronomy 18:15, 19)*

And from Acts...

> *For Moses said, 'The Lord your God will raise up for you a prophet like me from among your own people; you must listen to everything he tells you. Anyone who does not listen to him will be completely cut off from among his people.' (Acts 3:22-23)*

Notice the phrase, 'a prophet like me'. Contrary to virtually all Christian commentary, this is NOT Jesus. Jesus is not the prophet who 'prepares the way' for Jesus. To fulfill all righteousness (prophecy) John (the Baptist) prepared the way for Jesus. In his day, John was the wilderness prophet, not Jesus.

Also, Jesus is not formally a Prophet, he is an Apostle.

> *Wherefore, holy brethren, partakers of the heavenly calling, consider the Apostle and High Priest of our profession, Christ Jesus... (Hebrews 3:1 KJV)*

A kingdom must have apostles and prophets, two distinct ministries, and two distinct authorities – they are not interchangeable. These two ministries must operate in a legal separation-of-powers mode. The law-executer (President) is not legally allowed to be a law-maker (Senator) at the same time (in the U.S.). They are legally disparate. Jesus cannot legally be 'the prophet'.

It is also good to note how Jesus warns us about the false kingdom:

For _false Christs_ and _false prophets_ will appear and perform great signs and miracles to deceive even the elect—if that were possible. (Matthew 24:24)

Even the antichrist, an apostolic ministry, must have a prophet.

Again, the testimony of **Elijah** will be clear. The whole world knows the prophet is speaking for God. He has simply repeated a process taken right out of the pages of Scripture and he is obeying a direct command of Jesus (Matthew 24:14). He has asked the world to do the 'first commandment of the kingdom' – observe the Passover. Everyone should know this is the work of God.

The Last Passover

The gospel-of-the-kingdom, which includes the call for a Passover, confronts the world with the reality of 'God's will on earth'. It confronts the world (even the Christian world) with the truth. Dear reader, does this sound like God to you? Does the Christian world really think these instructions are obsolete in the twenty-first century? That God will try something totally new to institute the kingdom? (God used Passover to begin Christianity and then abolished it?)

This kingdom Passover is a one-of-a-kind- unique Passover. A Passover we will call the 'Last Passover'. We say last because it ends one world and starts the next.

Life is a journey. It typically has a number of stages. As the leading edge of spiritual humanity matures, there are major transition seasons; major passages from one stage to the next. The Day of Pentecost was one such day 2000 years ago. Today, the children have grown up, the world, in the name of these children, is near its Bar Mitzvah; it's the season of passage from childhood to adulthood.

The world is slowly heading toward the kingdom, and a world without sin and suffering—a world of peace and prosperity. It will be Paradise again! But the nature of Paradise is often misunderstood. Paradise is not the ultimate zoo for mankind, a place where God provides every conceivable delight (except freedom). Or worse yet, would be a Paradise maintained by robotic obedience.

No, God's ultimate plan is much more noble. Through a process of testing and choice, man, some men, will arise out of the mass of humanity, and become like God. They will not do this apart from God, but in God. Through the indwelling of the very Spirit of God, their thinking and ultimately their actions will conform to the perfection of God. That is what 'being made in the image of God' infers.

The kingdom is not imposed on all men, it is apprehended by some men. Forcefully apprehended, and then graciously extended for the blessing of others. The eternal kingdom is a two-tiered, two people group, kingdom. We will explain that more in "Chapter 10: MISSING THE OBVIOUS—THREE PEOPLE GROUPS".

But first we must talk about the end of this world, and what a born-again world may look like. We must have a 'Last Passover', and that can only come through human initiative. A fragment of humanity (as a mustard seed), as a prophetic spark, will speak a new and final message to this present world. That group will come to understand the prophetic process by which God intends to bring about that change, and they will become the very agents of that transition. The earth's **hard service** is nearly over, the 'good news of the kingdom' must be preached to the whole world as a testimony before the 'end' will come.

Chapter Nine

BUILDING A BORN-AGAIN WORLD (The End of the World)

'The end of the world', and 'the end of **hard service**', are synonymous with Jesus' words declaring 'the end' in Matthew 24:14. What you understand and believe about this term 'the end', will determine your prophecy, or perhaps, your prophecy will determine what you believe about 'the end'. Correct understanding of 'the end' is a phenomenon virtually absent in modern prophecy. But the world as we know it is going to end, soon. Seriously! And its death, as a seed, will give birth to a new world-order, known Biblically as 'the kingdom'.

To gauge the significance of this event, we can turn to Paul as he declares what 'the whole creation' is waiting for. What do you think Paul is going to say?

> *The creation waits in eager expectation for the sons of God to be revealed (Romans 8:19).*

To understand the kingdom properly we must shake off the idea that God or the Messiah is going to come and set it up initially. It certainly is the work of God, done by the power of God, but it can only be implemented by human initiative.

Our earlier statement bears repeating, the kingdom is not imposed on all men; it must, however, be apprehended by some men, forcefully and intentionally apprehended, organically. In other words, it becomes known and understood through an organic maturing process. A life process; becoming an adult. The kingdom comes in the manner of a proud father eagerly entrusting his business to his apprenticed (newly adult) sons.

Messiah as king comes, 'TO a kingdom'; 'TO a bride without spot or wrinkle'; 'TO a spiritual house', already functioning. But it is the prophet who comes first to initiate the final (adult) phases of those spiritual agencies and put the kingdom world in order. And, ironically, a new world-order begins with 'the end'.

The strategy of transformation has already been revealed in the pages of Scripture. The governance, the principles, and the righteousness of this kingdom, has been revealed and demonstrated in human history and in the pages of Scripture. It's as if all of human history has been preparing for this moment. Have we been paying attention?

Think about it. What if you and your group were given absolute power to implement this kingdom on earth? What would it look like? What would be the laws, the social structures, and the governance you would enforce upon the whole world to establish an enduring messianic age of righteousness, peace, and prosperity? Are you confident enough in your view of reality (God's reality), and truth, that you could handle such a responsibility?

How much effort in prayer, study, and discussion have we spent directed toward the kingdom on earth? Are we preparing for such a task? Or have our efforts been focused on 'going to heaven', and bringing as many as possible with us?

For most Christians, beyond living righteously, that is what Christian life is all about, isn't it? For them, this world is only a poor shadow of the joys of heaven. They need to review the end of the Book. Heaven is coming to earth. God (via the Temple—us) will dwell among men. Why is that necessary? The shocking prophetic truth is that none of that will even begin to happen until the people of earth say '*blessed is he who comes in the name of the Lord*' (Mathew 23:39). There will be no heavenly kingdom until there is an earthly kingdom.

Effectively, this is what the program is: humans, a worthy group of humans, will create the government of a new paradise, a structure for a much more complex world than Eden. It is a world reset to kingdom specs, an enforced clean start for the people of earth.

God created an environment 6000 years ago for two people. It is now time for some of their descendants to create a more permanent society for billions of people. There will be a reset of the world and a new and fuller revelation of God. With that established, the first generation of the Millennium (kingdom) will begin. In this new environment, new possibilities for good and evil will present themselves. Three identities will quickly manifest and mature, ending incredibly, in a falling away and rebellion (2 Thessalonians 2:3). The 'revealing of the sons of God' will directly lead to the revealing of the 'sons of the devil', and the 'sons of man'.

The Biblical Passover / Exodus was designed by the creator to trigger this transition. One world dies and another world is born. That is the background story of the Exodus. In the Passover, we have the spiritual underpinnings of personal salvation. Death, burial, and resurrection—to be born-again. So also, the death, burial, and resurrection of a born-again world.

At first, the process may seem shocking. The world will be given a clear 'last call' message. That message will include the demand for a one-time, global, Exodus-type Passover. Yes, there will be real households, with real lambs and real blood on the doorposts. This is how the kingdom starts.

The penalty for defying the Passover command is also taken from the pages of Scripture—the death of the firstborn. All the 'firstborns' on earth who defy this command will die. This is a critical part of the Exodus.

Who are the firstborns? There is still room for clarification and debate, but this would certainly include physical firstborn males, and likely 'spiritual firstborns' also, since Christianity is called the 'church of the firstborn' (Hebrews 12:23). All firstborns, defiant, apathetic, or willfully ignorant, will die, perhaps animals also.

Imagine what this could mean. Overnight, perhaps 500 million people die. Not in some drawn-out war or disease, but virtually instantly (for no apparent reason). This tragedy is close to home. Everyone loses neighbors, friends or family. It is a catastrophe unlike anything the earth has ever seen or imagined.

There is both a spiritual, as well as a psychological component to this apocalypse. Biblically, the firstborn is spiritually and symbolically distinct, representing the first power of the parents. The firstborn is the first of a new generation, collectively they represent the continuation of human society.

Killing the firstborn, those who defy the kingdom, is effectively killing the non-kingdom world, what we could refer to as the end of that world (system). The wheat and the tares have been separated; falsity has been cleansed from the body of Messiah. People of hope and faith can now give rise to a new world—the kingdom.

Shock and Awe

It is quite easy to see the spiritual design of the firstborn. But how does that translate into a new world. What could psychologically and emotionally prepare the world to yield to the kind of radical transformation we are talking about here? Human will is strong. How can the world's will be broken long enough to affect such a radical personality change?

Short of robotic reprogramming (God could do that), or massive, bloody conquest, there is only one mechanism known to man that could affect such a new-world-order for seven-plus billion people—an Exodus.

The Exodus is the only device known to man that can divide the old-world people from the new-world people AND provide the emotional shock and awe to pacify the survivors. The literal death of perhaps 500 million people overnight, and perhaps billions of animals, will have the required impact. We have a picture of just such an event in Scripture:

> *"As in the days when you came out of Egypt, I will show them my wonders." Nations will see and be ashamed, deprived of all their power. They will put their hands over their mouths and their ears will become deaf. They will lick dust like a snake, like creatures that crawl on the ground. They will come trembling out of their dens; they will turn in fear to the LORD our God and will be afraid of you. (Micah 7:15-17)*

Notice, the world surrenders! The new-world survivors, in fear and shock, turn to God, the God of Israel. Calling the world to repentance and to recognize the one true God has been the goal of Christian evangelism from its beginning. Finally, it has happened. The prophet and company, disciples of Jesus, through the prophetic Exodus, have now conquered the world for God. What evangelism couldn't finish directly, shock and awe did.

> *But I have raised you [Pharaoh] up for this very purpose, that I might show you my power and that my name might be proclaimed in all the earth. (Exodus 9:16)*

The Death of Christianity

But ironically, the success of the Christian message is also the end of its mission as we have known it. The first outcome of the Exodus will be a purging of Christianity itself—the death of Christianity's 'tares', its counterfeit members. The Exodus is the direct fulfilment of a parable Jesus taught, commonly called the Wheat and the Tares (Matthew. 13:24-30, 36-43). Judgement has begun at the house of the Lord. The Tares are dead, the (true) 'sons of God' are revealed. All of creation has been waiting for this event.

Effectively, the Christianity the world has known, its evangelistic message and its services, is now dead. From here on we'll call believers in Jesus the 'sons of God' (SOG) to distinguish them from the old institution of Christianity. The SOG will now leave the world and retreat into the 'wilderness'. Effectively the SOG are dead to this world. All material, relational, and legal connections to this world are effectively severed. They are truly 'in the world', but not 'of the world' (John 17).

Details at this point are not so important, but imagine shutting down and/or transferring management of ALL Christian institutions and ministries. All Christian churches, ministries, missions, schools, hospitals, headquarters, etc. (assuming they are truly Christian) effectively cease earthly activity as Christian institutions. True Christianity, the SOG, disappear from the world system.

One can imagine pseudo-Christian institutions continuing to function, and the emergence of more and more non-Biblical, and non-Christ-known ('I never knew you') institutions and 'ministries' perhaps even using the Christian name. In light of these harsh demands, it is likely, even a majority of Christian institutions today will be shown to be 'tares'. Regardless, the wheat and the tares will be separated, and the true Christ-knowns will leave the world.

They weren't 'raptured'; they were 'revealed', and sent into the wilderness directed towards a new and greater purpose. Falsity has been removed from Christianity leaving a truly pure and unified faith.

One can only try to imagine the complex process of liquidating the institutional, as well as the personal wealth, material possessions, and legal encumbrances of hundreds of millions of Christians as they leave the 'world'. The original Exodus pattern indicates the Israelites left their world with great wealth, much of which was given by those left behind.

We can begin to see what it means for the kingdom to come. And this will be relatively simple compared to what is going to happen next. The sons of God will largely disappear from earthly activities for a generation, a period for as long as forty years. When their period of transformation is over, they, a new generation, will reappear on the world stage as a glorious corporate body we are referring to as '*Joseph*' (in Matthew 24:45), and begin a *Joseph* ministry, the second commission.

Transforming the World

With the bulk of the sons of God company in the 'wilderness', the prophet and team will turn in earnest to the business of transforming the world. The world has just seen the true God of heaven, his prophet(s), and his people speaking with power and truth. The world's gods, false religions, and philosophies such as Humanism, Atheism. Evolutionism, Materialism, Marxism, and any number of other isms have been crushed along with any overt resistance to the Exodus. The world is impressed, confused, and still very much in a state of shock. It is the perfect moment for transformation.

The prophet is in effect a (benevolent) one-world dictator, probably still with absolute divine power, if needed. Now is the moment to strike. It is time to legally and socially reorganize the world into structures and cultures compatible with the kingdom.

As we have stated a number of times before, the exact details, limits, and implementation of this transformation is not so important at this stage. What is important is a general understanding of what is happening on earth. The earth with its billions of people is being reset. It is being reset according to the principles of justice, equality, and righteousness; into a world that everyone should have wanted, but didn't; a world where those gifted to be leaders should affirm justice for all, rather than self-serving advantage. A new world demanding of its people personal responsibility and righteousness.

One important factor is trust. The people of earth can trust the prophet. As a member of the sons of God, he and his whole people group have (permanently) separated themselves from the things of this world. They are citizens of heaven, never again to gather and enjoy the material things of this earth for themselves. As a community, they have 'all things in common', living as a royal priesthood.

Because of this, the world can trust the prophet to operate in their collective best interest. It should be noted here that perhaps a majority of the people of earth have not had significant spiritual transformations. And while a massive external transformation is taking place to align the world with godly principles, both socially and legally, it does not mean the world's people have personally embraced all those principles.

This first stage of the kingdom does not produce heaven on earth. It is just a first step in that direction. The mechanics of the kingdom and the truth of its superiority is given to the world. The prophet will enforce the principles that make for peace and justice, but the shock and awe will soon wear off. The prophet, with a new-world-order largely complete, will retreat to the wilderness with the sons of God, and too much of the world will slowly return to their old ways. The world is now given time to decide for itself, 'whom will we serve'. The full *Restoration* requires a generation and a second major operation before it is complete; ending with the coming of Messiah as king.

Filling the Void

With Christianity essentially removed from the world, something must fill the spiritual void. That something, which will slowly become the first 'religion' of earth is Torah Judaism (a Judaism that truly follows the Torah), the spiritual roots of Christianity.

The prophet will encourage and support the establishment of the Levitical priesthood and the authoritative role of the Sanhedrin. Earlier, these entities (Priests) would have likely led the world in the Exodus Passover sacrifice on the Temple Mount in Jerusalem. The role of the prophet and the sons of God will be to ascribe dignity and honor to the new (native) spiritual leaders of earth. The world will come up to Jerusalem to learn the ways of God.

This is what the Lord Almighty says: "In those days ten men from all languages and nations will take firm hold of one Jew by the hem of his robe and say, 'Let us go with you, because we have heard that God is with you.' " (Zechariah. 8:23)

Extending out of a Torah theology will come a new governance on earth. Why Torah theology? Rightly understood and applied, Torah is God's perfect revelation of righteousness to mankind. First given to Israel at Mt. Sinai, the New Testament calls it '*the embodiment of knowledge and truth*' (Romans. 2:20). The Torah reflects the true nature of God, and over time, it was intended to be extended to the whole world. Rightly applied it is the perfect model of righteousness, and there is no other such model given to mankind.

Over 1500 years, Israel translated the constitution given at Sinai into law which was affirmed as perfect by the expression of the perfect life of the Son of God.

But when the time had fully come, God sent his Son, born of a woman, born under law, (Galatians 4:4)

Christian theology, as it is today, is not workable in this new world. It was shaped for a different purpose. To penetrate the pagan world, Christianity created an 'abbreviated Judaism' mixed with the spiritual elements of the 'new creation' made available by Jesus, and added some assorted pagan elements along the way. In that, it has been successful. Through Jesus, one third of earth's humanity claim to have chosen the gracious offer of salvation (really redemption) offered by him. But Christianity has veered away from the full theology and lifestyle of its Jewish founders.

The benefits to the world have been immense, and certainly part of God's progressive sovereign work. Largely through Christianity, the Scriptures and the knowledge of the God of Abraham has permeated the world and its cultures. Western Civilization in particular embodies a strong Christian influence.

One clear example of that Christian influence is how time is referenced throughout the world. Think about it. In ancient times, large civilizations or kingdoms would establish a time-reference based upon a notable king or major event. The world had many ways to mark time. Here's just a few examples from the Bible:

- In the twelfth year of Ahaz king of Judah... (2Ki 17:1 KJV)
- And it came to pass in the fourth year of king Hezekiah... (2Ki 18:9 KJV)
- But in the eighteenth year of king Josiah... (2Ki 23:23 KJV)
- And it came to pass, [that] in the fifth year of king Rehoboam Shishak king of Egypt... (2Ch 12:2 KJV)
- Now in the eighteenth year of king Jeroboam... (2Ch 13:1 KJV)
- In the year that king Uzziah died... (Isa 6:1 KJV)

Imagine an ancient 'World History' book. How would it reference time over centuries. It would be chaotic. So many disciplines would be mind-numbingly complicated if they existed at all. How could the physical and social sciences develop? How would one teach the sciences of archeology, anthropology, or geology without a uniform reference to time? How would knowledge of human civilization be transmitted? We absolutely take for granted the benefits of a uniform reference to time.

So, how did we get one? Which king, or which event in history, is worthy of a universal reference to time? The world has spoken. There is only one man who has the standing to become earth's reference for time. A man, who was born in a barn to a poor family, who likely never traveled more than a few hundred miles from home. A man who never held a public office, who never wrote a single page (that we have a record of), and who was tortured and martyred before he was forty.

Yet, this is the man the world accepts as worthy of being the time-reference for human history. Today, virtually every reference to time, from every social, scientific, or religious discipline, uses this man, Jesus, as their reference. How can we explain this other than the sovereign work of God? And there is even more to this strange story.

A Message in Time

The world chose well! And because they chose this man, God can now speak more directly and specifically. God will reveal himself and more of his truth (reality) through the medium of time.

Many of us can remember the decade leading up to Y2K, the year 2000. For years, especially the last few years leading up to the year 2000, Y2K was constantly in the headlines. A dark cloud was menacing human civilization.

Many were shouting, 'The world was going to shut down' (or something to that effect). Because of some long-standing technical accommodation, the world's digital computer systems were going to fail. At the tick of the first second of the year 2000, the world's computer systems would malfunction and fail—no finances, no transportation, no food, no gas, no communications, no electricity, etc. This was the worst-case scenario proclaimed around the world leading up to Y2K.

Could this worldwide techno-crisis have any spiritual message? Could this be God speaking? Yes! Since the world had no prominent prophets yet, God spoke a prophetic message through computer programmers. What was this critical message leading up to the year 2000?

Think Sabbath! Yes, the Sabbath millennium was about to start. What is the nature of Sabbath? Rest! Stop what you have been doing and rest. Normal commerce stops for a moment. Through this message, God was giving us a troubling hint about the next millennium, the seventh millennium. God was saying, in a rather unconventional way, the kingdom is coming, it will not be business as usual. Sabbath(s) will now be critical to the earth's future. This was a message Christianity was not able to deliver at that time.

If they had, the earth would have known that if one prepares, the Sabbath is refreshing and glorious. However, if one does not, it can be discomforting, or even catastrophic in a prophetic sense. In fact, there are two major 'Sabbath' events in the earth's prophetic future (only one is covered in some detail in this book).

For those interested in the technical reasons behind this prophetic message, ask a techie. But very briefly, here is a short explanation. Computer programmers of the 1950's and 1960's mainframes (that's all there were then), because computer memory was very expensive and therefore limited, used only two digits to store the year in the world's databases and communications—1960 was abbreviated as 60. When the computer pulled out the year digits (60), it would always assume to add 1900. The engineers were dealing with an immediate issue, not thinking far enough ahead. What happens when the world's computer clocks roll over from year 99 to year 00. Computer networks and processing will think they are back at 1900; or some will and some won't. Disaster ensues!

Computer networks and embedded systems all over the world would malfunction, or so the experts warned us for the decade leading up to Y2K. They warned, planes would fall out of the sky, commerce would be disrupted, computers won't be able to talk to each other, our technology-dependent world will tragically break down and stop.

The whole world held its breath as midnight December 31, 1999 approached. With hearts thrilled to be personally entering a new millennium (how often does that happen?), many prepared to celebrate. In crisis mode, the world had spent many millions of dollars to fix the problem, or so they hoped. As the night approached, most of the world was cautiously optimistic. They would celebrate while keeping one eye on the news.

So it was, that every time-zone on earth planned for, and celebrated Y2K, the arrival of year 2000. But many, perhaps most, didn't stop to wonder, 'Two thousand years since what?' Why all the fireworks, what were we all celebrating? Who determined that on this date the world would slide into a new millennium anyway?

Christian authorities had! Approximately 15 centuries earlier Christian authorities made the birth of Jesus Christ the dividing point of their world. And as we said, over time the world came to agreed (even without full understanding).

The whole world celebrated. It was two thousand years since the birth of Jesus, earth's most significant Son. He ALONE has the standing to become earth's reference for time, BC and AD, time before his life, and time after. [And by the way, using the 'significant son' is how God marks time. Check out Genesis 5]

And because the world chose him, the world was now being enlightened to God's prophetic program. Now we know, because of this proper time-reference, that human history is entering the Sabbath millennium. Any other time-reference would not have given us that revelation. The world, even while unaware, is slowly conforming to the nature and will of God.

Righteousness in Fact

Part of this new world-order, is a new place for Christianity. For instance, Christianity is not the best teacher of a seventh day Sabbath. They long ago abandoned it. Also, while Christianity has focused on a 'righteousness by faith' and 'the kingdom of heaven', rightly so, the kingdom on earth, if it is to be successful, must possess righteousness-in-fact. The kingdom on earth cannot be based on the Christian foundational concept called 'justification' (a legal righteousness). No, there must be actual righteous behavior, true righteous behavior between God and man, and man and man. In this earthly kingdom, what you believe is not enough. Faith must produce works, eventually perfect works.

The Christian 'gospel' (of salvation) is not designed for this task. In this new world, the simple fact is, much of Christian theology, and its 'born-again salvation', will no longer be directly relevant to earth. Christianity has retreated into the wilderness along with much of its theology. Christian salvation is over. What is left, and vital for the world at large, are the roots of Christian theology, Torah Judaism (initially, less the Temple, etc.).

The seeds of the kingdom have been sown and cultivated, but a new formality must now be imposed upon the world. Through the Exodus event mentioned earlier, the world has effectively been conquered. And as in any conquered land, the conquering force may invalidate existing laws and dictate new laws. The big difference here is that this kingdom change is for the benefit of the conquered not the conquering.

What the world needs now is a new society built from the ground up, both the children and legal systems being instilled with the righteousness and ethics of God's revelation, as taught by the earthly priesthood. The destination is no longer heaven, but heaven on earth. And that will take some time.

Jubilee - the Year of the Lord's Favor

The prophets of Israel revealed a time of renewal as described in this book. The Gospel of Luke includes one such account of Jesus reading from Isaiah and applying it to his ministry:

> *The scroll of the prophet Isaiah was handed to him. Unrolling it, he found the place where it is written: "The Spirit of the Lord is on me, because he has anointed me to preach good news to the poor. He has sent me to proclaim freedom for the prisoners and recovery of sight for the blind, to release the oppressed, to proclaim the year of the Lord's favor." (Luke 4:17-19)*

Yes, the year of the Lord's favor was proclaimed and is coming soon, a Jubilee. Earth's rulers, and the systems they have created, have not always been kind to earth's meek and lowly. God has prepared a time to rebalance the scales of justice.

The Biblical idea of 'Jubilee' is a type of this 'world renewal' we are describing here. A kingdom model would have regular jubilees (every 49 years), in which there are personal resets, and everyone is guaranteed their original homestead, with debts canceled, etc. To start a system like this requires an initial clean start. A baseline from which growing inequities, greater or lesser, can be rebalanced. To do this it requires an initial equal distribution of resources—land, wealth, etc.

Jesus proclaimed this good news, but his life was cut short. It is now up to the sons of God, the Body of Jesus (the Bride of Messiah), to continue his work. Again, from Isaiah:

> *"Every valley shall be exalted, and every mountain and hill shall be made low: and the crooked shall be made straight, and the rough places plain:" (Isaiah 40:4 KJV).*

It is now time to establish an earthly governance that will do just that. This will take a great deal of wisdom and time. We find a framework for this transformation in the Torah concept of Jubilee, and in the account of settling of the Promised Land in the days of Joshua.

Again, the exact details are not important here, and there is room for debate, but here are some of the key transformations the new world will likely require. It's not magical. It will take the wisdom of God and the council of skilled minds to implement these very complex reforms.

So, where do we start?

World Government Begins in the Family:

The new kingdom world will not be dependent upon top-heavy, inefficient, and corrupting government, but rather strong and revitalized two parent family and extended family units. Starting from the bottom up, the first task is to certify or create authoritative family units. The Christian Old Testament (in their order of books, the last book is Malachi), so appropriately closes with this prophetic summary:

> *Remember the Law of Moses my servant ... Behold, I will send you Elijah THE PROPHET ... And he shall turn the hearts of the*

fathers to the children, and the hearts of the children to their fathers... (Malachi 4:4-6)

These words capture the essence of end time prophecy and the *Restoration.*

Biblical Israel society was tribal and patriarchal. So too, the basic building block of kingdom society must be the patristic (male led) clan. Local responsibility and support is the first level of government. Everyone must belong; either genealogically or initially by deliberate assignment to some family unit. Every person on earth will be known and assigned to some functioning, governing family unit. Every human on earth (ideally) will be a card carrying, accountable member of some family. There will be no lost sheep.

World government must begin at home, a binding family unit where the first level of nurturing, provision, education, care, accountability, and discipline is dispensed and available to all members. This is where a new world must start. The kingdom must cultivate responsible people, molded in righteousness, and accountable to the greater good.

Amnesty and Healing:

Beyond the general population, this 'family-forming' task must extend out to the fringe elements of society. The good news of the kingdom is especially good news to the most-needy members of society. Those segments, as noted by Luke 4 above, include the poor, the prisoners, the sick, and the spiritually oppressed.

Jesus foreshadowed this ministry in his own. Here are some examples:

While they were going out, a man who was demon-possessed and could not talk was brought to Jesus. And when the demon was driven out, the man who had been mute spoke. The crowd was amazed and said, "Nothing like this has ever been seen in Israel." (Matthew 9:32-33)

Jesus went through all the towns and villages, teaching in their synagogues, preaching the good news of the kingdom and healing every disease and sickness. (Matthew 9:35)

He called his twelve disciples to him and gave them authority to drive out evil spirits and to heal every disease and sickness. (Matthew 10:1)

As you go, preach this message: 'The kingdom of heaven is near.' Heal the sick, raise the dead, cleanse those who have leprosy, drive out demons. Freely you have received, freely give. (Matthew 10:7-8)

The dawn of a new day has come. What was rehearsed 2000 years ago is now pouring forth into the whole world. A special day, a time of new beginnings. Flowing from a work completed on Calvary by Jesus, the mercies of God can now be poured out in even greater streams. We see these times of favor prefigured in the Torah concepts of Shemitah and Jubilee (the seven and fifty-year releases), and also the prophetic Sabbath which is commonly referred to by Christianity as the Millennium.

The burden of sin has been heavy for mankind, and the testimony of God's love has not always been so clear to everyone. Innocence may be pled on behalf of the guilty; broken families, corrupting communities, ignorance, alienation, and persecution may warrant grace. Surely some, perhaps many, were not previously given a compelling view of the path of peace. This is a unique moment of compassion and mercy.

It is a time of reconciliation like never before. Justice must begin by erring on the side of mercy. The whole world has received a clear testimony, and now knows the God of Israel and his Son. The day calls for unilateral forgiveness echoed in a voice from our past...

"...neither do I condemn you... go and sin no more" (John 8:11)

Now, with new world clarity and accountability, the debts of mankind can be forgiven.

"All have sinned and fallen short..." (Romans 2:23)

The mercy of God, including forgiveness, is part of the ministry of reconciliation, given to men (the priesthood).

But that ye may know that the Son of man hath power on earth to forgive sins, (then saith he to the sick of the palsy,) Arise, take up thy bed, and go unto thine house. And he arose, and departed to his house. But when the multitudes saw [it], they marvelled, and glorified God, which had given such power unto men. (Matthew 9:6-8 KJV)

The gift of grace flowing from the wounds of the Lamb of God can certainly offer this one-time amnesty to the world. The prophet, in Jesus' name, will declare the sins of all mankind forgiven.

This amnesty will likely extend even to those imprisoned by literal chains and bars. All the world's prisoners will likely be freed and also restored to functioning families (and accompanied by serious accountability).

This is peace on earth and good will to men. A new world must start with individuals, and as we can see, it certainly will. Perhaps there will even be total healing of all sick or injured. Sins forgiven, prisoners freed, health restored, families reconciled, this is the start of a new creation. But wait, there is even more good news.

Equality - Wealth and Real-Estate

Every free man must have a home, a place to put his name. Adam had his garden in the first creation. The new world must provide the same. Each man must also have his own garden, his personal piece of the new world.

But they shall sit every man under his vine and under his fig tree; and none shall make [them] afraid: for the mouth of the LORD of hosts hath spoken [it]. [Micah 4:4 KJV]

So, it would seem that there must be some mechanism to equalize wealth and real-estate. Dividing the land among families was part of the Israelite program after they had entered and conquered the Promised Land.

Too often in this current world, wealth has not been gained fairly. Advantage may not necessarily come from the barrel of a gun or illegally. Advantage may come through unjust laws, rigged associations, or even unethical (but legal) application of permissible standards.

This is not an indictment of the wealthy. Often enough, the wealthy are the super producers of a society, especially in 'free' societies. It should be noted that being 'poor' does not automatically convey any sense of superior righteousness, nor does being 'rich' convey any sense of inferior righteousness.

Black or gray, fair or not, it is time to start fresh. If we have been blessed or oppressed it is time that…

"Every valley shall be exalted, and every mountain and hill shall be made low."

In theory, at least, it is time to create a level playing field. Here again, this will be extremely complex and will require the wisdom of Solomon to execute a righteous plan of equalization of both wealth and real-estate. Again, the details are not so important here.

Essentially all the wealth and eligible land on earth will need to be distributed equally to family groups. What an awesome plan of blessing and prosperity. In addition, this land division scheme must be initialized for the concept of Jubilee to function where no one can lose their original homestead.

Class warfare should be a thing of the past. The gospel of victimization, of identity politics, and the gospel of all socialistic authoritarian regimes, will be overcome. Animosity, envy, and distrust will be suppressed, at least for a season. New and wonderful possibilities are breaking forth on earth. Every noble man and woman should understand the benefits of this plan for human civilization. What more could possibly be done to manifest the hope of 'peace on earth, and good will toward men'.

Nations and Languages

But there is at least one more structural correction that needs to be implemented to set the world in order. Family clans have been rebuilt and supplied with an initial inheritance and homestead. This is where government needs to start. But there is a place for associations and expressions beyond clans or tribes—we call them nations. National expressions are formed by common language, culture, ethnicity, and history.

There are nearly 200 nations on earth at the beginning of the twenty first century. And there are roughly 6,500 spoken languages in the world today. However, about 2,000 of those languages have fewer than 1,000 speakers.

An interesting side note regarding languages and Bible translations: Wycliffe Global Alliance reports that as of 2015 at least one book of Scripture exists in over 2,900 of these languages. And the 'Vision 2025 Resolution' declares, "We embrace the vision that by the year 2025 a Bible translation project will be in progress for every people group that needs it."

In many cases a nation is characterized by a distinct language. In many other cases, nations and their boundaries have been arbitrarily imposed by larger world bodies. For humanity, nation-building and language dissemination has been somewhat arbitrary and/or contrived.

It would seem that a new world might require a more deliberate and beneficial dissemination of nations and languages.

As we might assume, the Bible and spiritual tradition has a lot to say about this issue of nations and languages. God, the creator of heaven and earth, apparently has a more deliberate and beneficial order to the nationalistic design of earth. Paul pointed in this direction when he spoke to the world's elite in his day:

> *Paul then stood up in the meeting of the Areopagus and said: "People of Athens! ... From one man he made all the nations, that they should inhabit the whole earth; and he marked out their appointed times in history and the boundaries of their lands. (Acts 17:22,26 NIV)*

Genesis gives us the early formation of man and human society. After the cleansing of the flood, humanity starts again:

> *This is the account of Shem, Ham and Japheth, Noah's sons, who themselves had sons after the flood. ... These are the clans of Noah's sons, according to their lines of descent, within their nations. From these the nations spread out over the earth after the flood. [Genesis 10:1, 3]*

In this Chapter 10, post-flood account, we have what is often called "The Table of Nations." It lists 70 (or 72) ethnic groups that dispersed around the world, likely from the Tower of Babel. It was at the tower of Babel that God divided the languages of earth. In the next Chapter, Genesis 11, we have the account of the Tower of Babel:

> *Now the whole world had one language and a common speech. As men moved eastward, they found a plain in Shinar and settled there. They said to each other, "Come, let's make bricks and bake them thoroughly." They used brick instead of stone, and tar for mortar. Then they said, "Come, let us build ourselves a city, with a tower that reaches to the heavens, so that we may make a name for ourselves and not be scattered over the face of the*

whole earth." But the Lord came down to see the city and the tower that the men were building. The Lord said, "If as one people speaking the same language they have begun to do this, then nothing they plan to do will be impossible for them. Come, let us go down and confuse their language so they will not understand each other." So the Lord scattered them from there over all the earth, and they stopped building the city. That is why it was called Babel - because there the Lord confused the language of the whole world. From there the Lord scattered them over the face of the whole earth. (Genesis 11:1-9)

The following excerpt is from biblebelievers.org on "Genesis 10 – the Table of Nations". It is their analysis of the role of language in both dividing mankind, and also expressing the unique creative potentials God created within mankind that is very interesting (the underlined emphasis is ours).

"Philology," which is the science of the structure and development of language, has discovered three parent groups of languages and peoples: Aryan, Semitic, and Turanian (who are Asiatic and neither Aryan nor Semitic)—Japheth, Shem, and Ham. Family traits are evident in the languages of the different groups <u>as language determines or reflects the way men conceive of things.</u>

The Japhetic or the Indo-Europeans have maintained the evident relationships in their particular family of languages. And the same observation applies to the Semitic languages. Even though they have spread so widely, <u>they have continued to share a certain way of viewing things</u>. Indo-Europeans <u>philosophically with an emphasis on the abstract</u>, and the Semites with their <u>emphasis upon behavior</u> from a more transendential point of view.

From all over the world, wherever Ham and Canaan are found, the witness is to <u>an entirely practical view of the world</u>, rooted in the present, wise in a canny sort of way, specific, particular, <u>uninterested in the abstract, always inventing new words or new</u>

terms for things, interested in particulars rather than categories,
earthy, and very largely disinterested in unlikely possibilities.

The family of the Indo-European languages is readily identifiable
as a family, as are the Semitic tongues. The Hamites, however,
have been so inventive, they devise terms with equal facility and
their languages are in such a state of flux that within a few
generations, even tribes living just across the river will find
themselves scarcely able to converse.

This strange tendency which has prevented the Egyptians,
Hittites, Sumerians, Chinese and Central American Indians from
developing an alphabetical script may have been Providence,
guaranteeing the quick dispersal of Ham all over the world.
Many cuniform scholars have noted the similarities between
Sumarian and Chinese. "Civilization has traveled with the sun,
from the east, coming west... The oldest civilization is China, ...
And sin has traveled with civilization" (We Have Seen His Star
and Have Come to Worship Him, 28:188).

What divided the Hamites in this way was not a difference in
language structure, for the philosophy of their languages
remained remarkably similar, so that the ways of thinking of the
African native, the Chinese peasant, and the American Indian
have remained for a very long time comparable: it was the
vocabularies which changed.

According to Genesis 10:32, the families of the sons of Noah are
divided or separated by languages into tribes and nations. These
boundaries also knit them together in their generic group. This
is a protective measure to ensure each people would be separate
yet interdependent in order to realize the maximum capacity of
man with his tremendous creative potential.

Any attempt to unify the world's language, to co-mingle the
races or nations with the overt intention of making all men share
equally in this potential will only serve to defeat its own purpose
in the end. Thus Esperanto, "multiculturalism", gender equality,
the UN, WCC and "the brotherhood of all mankind", are
artificial, in direct opposition to God's purposes, and in a manner

of speaking, a repetition of the hubris of Babel (Genesis 11:1-6;
Matthew 24:37-38).

Even in man's disobedience and rebellion, God's discipline and judgement is meant for good. The Table of Nations (Genesis 10) and the Tower of Babel (Genesis 11) point to a diverse, but limited, collection of nations with their unique language or dialect. The Table of Nations seems to indicate God's 'ideal' nation count to be a number near 70. That number is reinforced down through history. Here are some random quotes from an article on the website wikinoah.org - "Seventy Nations":

The Talmudic tradition that there are seventy language families in the world is based on the list of Noah's descendants [1]. This tradition of seventy (-two) meta-nations is deep-rooted. According to the Midrash each of the seventy nations is placed under the protection of a special angel, except Israel, whose Protector is G-d Himself. [2]

The seventy bullocks sacrificed on Tabernacles were offered to atone for the seventy nations. 'Woe to the nations!' says Rav Yochanan; 'for they suffered a loss [by having destroyed the Temple] and do not realize the extent of the loss. While the Temple existed the altar [the sacrifices] atoned for them, but now [that it is destroyed] who will atone for them?'[3]

According to many commentators[4] this concept seems to underlie Deut. 32:8 which says that G-d 'established the boundaries of nations [i.e. the seventy nations]... according to the number of the children of Israel' -- namely the seventy who descended to Egypt with Yakov [5]

The seventy members of the Sanhedrin also corresponded to the seventy nations of the world.[6] The Jewish law required that every member of the Sanhedrin should have sufficient knowledge of the seventy languages to be able to listen to testimony without an interpreter.[7]

The Torah was written in seventy languages in order that the nations should not be able to plead ignorance as their excuse for rejecting it.[12] Among the seventy languages the most noble is Hebrew, for in it was pronounced the creative word of G-d.[13]

Just as there were seventy nations[14], the words of the Torah engraved on the Tablets on Mount Ebal[15] were written in seventy languages[16] so that all the nations might read it. For the same reason, G-d's voice at Sinai divided itself into seventy languages.[17]

Each of the seventy nations represented a unique characteristic, as the Sages say, one excelled in warfare, another in licentiousness, another in beauty and so on. All of these national virtues and strains of character are present in Israel as well for each person has gifts to develop and temptations to overcome. G-d wants all nations to rise to their greatest spiritual potential.

These variations were present in the individuals of Jacob's family. And the seventy languages used by Moses parallel the seventy facets of Torah; each 'speaks' to one of the seventy characteristics with which G-d has populated the world. (It may also be suggested that each of the seventy offerings of Tabernacles atoned for the trespasses of each of these seventy national characteristics present within Israel, and consequently the nations of the world benefited from this universal atonement).

Israel, as the spiritual model of the world, was to demonstrate within itself that eminence is within reach of every nation; that every type of person can live a Torah life.

Therefore, a significant portion of Jewish life revolves around the number seventy to symbolize that every national trait can become harnessed for holy purposes.[20]

Early Christian writers also took the Table of Nations as determinant of the number of existing nations and languages. Also, Jesus apparently ordained a group of seventy (or seventy-two) apostles in addition to the twelve (Luke 10:1).

As we learned from the Tower of Babel account, unity (one language) can be a powerful force for good or evil. God, in his response to humanity's rebellious attempt at independence, recognized the wonderful and mysterious diversity of human personality and creativity.

Hidden within Adam, awaiting full expression, was not only the singularly beautiful mystery of Eve, but also the diversity of the full human personality. These personalities and creative potentials would slowly emerge through the lives of Noah and his three sons.

Diversity Abuse

There certainly is beauty in diversity. But diversity has a limit. God has a design that becomes apparent to all who are seeking to know his 'reality' (truth). We live in a day and culture in which men are seeking independence from God in the vilest ways. Human creativity is now used to invent new evils.

From time-immemorial (the Garden) there have been two sexes and one form of marriage. In our lifetime, we have seen this change. With creative word-plays and an abandonment of rational thinking (common sense), we now have same-sex marriage, transgender bathrooms, and 'sexual fluidity'.

As of 2014, Facebook lets U.S. users choose among 50 plus additional options such as "transgender," "cisgender," "gender fluid," "intersex" and "neither" to describe themselves. This is not human advancement but human abasement. This type of diversity is an affront to God, denying what a human is meant to be—the image of God.

> *So God created man in his own image, in the image of God he created him; male and female he created them. (Genesis 1:27)*

With the wisdom of God, expressed within the ministry of the sons of God, humanity will freely and thoughtfully determine where the boundaries are. It seems quite apparent that there are two sexes, 70 languages, and 70 nations. This is diversity at is best. This is the right balance between one and too many.

'*Adam*', in the guise of the manifested sons of God, is rightly continuing where the first Adam stumbled. He is now tending the garden again. This is what the whole creation has been eagerly waiting for. He is fulfilling his mandate—taking dominion over his creation, to serve and care for it in the best possible way. It is now far more complex, the journey has had many ups and downs, but the sovereign rule and purposes of God have not been thwarted in the least. In fact, the glory and majesty of God's idea of reality are now being fully manifested.

Instead of two in the garden, we have billions of couples with their own gardens, cultivated within a sustainable environment. [Caring for the physical earth was part of Adam's responsibility; the sons of God will surely institute common-sense environmental policies that balance human and environmental needs.]

In a very real sense, the kingdom has come to earth. The external structures of a perfect world have been initiated through Spirit-led human initiative. But the full potential of relationship with God has not permeated into the billions of citizens of earth. That personal relationship cannot be coerced as has many of the external kingdom transformations.

The kingdom is not perfected yet, but world government and family clans have been radically transformed to support the ultimate paradise. There is still good and evil clearly revealed in its essence, yet given liberty to find full expression in the hearts of people. This is God's intention. He will now give the world the time and liberty to raise a single generation in light of God's truth and mercy.

This is true of all human groups on earth. The sons of God have been separated from the 'world' and they have been given their own mandate to raise a perfect generation. The rest of humanity have not been clearly defined, but the fruit of their efforts will eventually become clear.

Jesus' mandate was to bring truth to the world and then division. The nature of this division of humanity, and the ultimate eternal categories or groups, has been hidden from Christianity. At this point in our overview the sons of God have made their choice; they have been set-apart, destined for perfection.

We have come to the harvest generation. Beyond the 'jubilee' graces given to the world, elements of the **hard service** (the Genesis curse) have also been lifted. There is a new freedom and a new power-environment designed to mature the 'fruit' of the human personality, in all its diversity, whether good or evil.

Who is this 'man' made in the image of God? He is an amalgamation of all human potential. We quickly see in Genesis that 'woman' was hidden in 'man' and needed to be separated. And again, after a long struggle, the sons of God have now been revealed and separated from 'man'. But man is not yet fully revealed. There are two more natures within him yet to be identified and divided. We will discuss the mystery of people groups next.

Chapter Ten

MISSING THE OBVIOUS—THREE PEOPLE GROUPS

In our short prophetic story of mankind, thus far, we have presented two radically new ideas. First, the unexpected role of human initiative and leadership with almost God-like access to revelation and power. We especially see this demonstrated in the role of 'the prophet' (**Elijah**), in managing the **Restoration**. And second, a radical process of rebuilding, reordering, and redistributing the world's families, languages, nations, wealth and real-estate. With this human directed process, the kingdom is literally taking root in the earth; God's will on earth is literally being done.

And just as these radical transformations to come have remained largely hidden from current prophetic study, the ultimate design and structure of the kingdom has also remained hidden.

Part of the reason for this is the human tendency to 'keep things simple'. Simplicity is a nice aspiration, but humans and God's kingdom are not ultimately so simple. As Albert Einstein once said, "*Everything should be made as simple as possible, but not simpler.*" Too simple has been positive for a season, but at some point, we have to deal with the full reality.

A more realistic understanding of the end-of-the-age is required to 'prepare' (identify and mature) three people groups, rather than two.

We will see that this idea is remarkably consistent throughout Scriptures, but it has not been seen for what it is. In the next four chapters we will do a quick survey of this three-people-group thread starting in Genesis. It is not possible to understand prophecy without understanding these three people groups, their function and purpose.

Heaven and Hell

Going back to Genesis again, we see...

"In the beginning God created the heavens and the earth"

The (Christian) Bible begins and ends with the emphasis on <u>heaven and earth</u>. Christianity, on the other hand, in its passion for evangelism, has effectively skewed the emphasis to <u>heaven and hell</u>. From their perspective there are only, 'the saints' and 'the aints'. There are two, and only two, eternal people groups. Effectively, every human who ever lived will either 'go to heaven' or 'go to hell'.

This simplicity has been fruitful, but it is not reality. Christianity has recognized only one commission, the 'Great Commission', and only an abbreviated gospel, the 'gospel of salvation', rather than the full 'gospel-of-the-kingdom'.

This single-minded passion to evangelize the world has been successful. The world has been given the Bible in almost 3000 languages; the gospel of salvation by grace, and compassion ministries like schools, hospitals, orphanages, and feeding programs have transformed the world.

The downside to sending the 'good news' of salvation to the pagan world has been the over-simplification and dumbing-down of God's full program of *restoration* for this world and its people. In particular, even the prophetic program has been adapted to the singular goal of evangelism.

"Where will you go when you die?" "How can I escape the coming judgement?" These are the leading motivations behind Christian prophecy today.

With this heaven and hell mentality gripping the Christian world, it is little wonder that it has missed the other two commissions found in Matthew 24. By not seeing the commissions, one will not likely see the objective of the two commissions—to divide and perfect three eternal people groups, rather than two. Heaven and hell, yes, but we have overlooked a serious program for earth.

With the mention of the three people groups, we have now, essentially reached the goal of Biblical prophecy. The end goal of current human history, in particular, the period we are calling the *Restoration*, the period before the Messiah comes (returns) to begin his literal reign, is to divide humanity into three eternal identity groups. This idea agrees with the words of Jesus:

> *Do you think I came to bring peace on earth? No, I tell you, but division. (Luke 12:51 NIV)*

The Millennium begins with the *Restoration* period, a one-generation process that identifies and matures each of the three people groups. The *Restoration* will have two filtering processes, one at the beginning and one immediately after the end. The Millennium will end with a third filtering process in preparation for the new heavens and the new earth.

The three groups are: Citizens of heaven (who are still on earth), who we will refer to as RULERS; citizens of earth (who are still on earth, who we will refer to as CITIZENS; and rebels (who are still on earth), who we will refer to as REBELS. (All the dead will eventually be connected with one of these groups forever). These living groups are formed through a generation-long program where each group is divided, tested, and begins to function in their eternal callings.

One can see how this might get a little complicated, and take a bit of time, unless God just snapped his finger and instantly everyone was marked and put in his place. But wait, that's how the world started; God just spoke and it happened. When it was over, God walked with Adam in the garden.

There was fellowship, but it seems God wanted, needed, and planned more for us. Now, God has able partners; and he wants them deeply involved in the act of (re)creating.

One can also see why the process of recreating the world, the *Restoration*, must be more complex and take longer—it must be a more natural process than the original creation, this time largely managed by humans. Our goal now is to identify and harvest three distinct identities. Previous to this, evangelical Christianity's goal was a 'harvest of souls'. The *Restoration* is designed to achieve a 'harvest of righteousness' (or character).

What follows below will be an extensive but brief survey of the 'three-people-groups' woven into human history as revealed in the pages of Scripture. But, first let's review the three categories.

RULERS - Sons of God

Christianity is a 'faith' centered on its founder, best known today, as Jesus Christ or Jesus the Messiah. In its original form, Christianity was a product, or sect, of Judaism. While Judaism of Jesus' day was centered on the Temple and Priesthood, and Israel's promised territory, the kingdom of David, Christianity's scope is much larger. Christianity was more mystical and more universal, emphasizing the 'kingdom of heaven' rather than the 'Royal House of David'.

Jesus, and the Apostolic founders did not advocate a political or militaristic body or church (although Christianity was in no way pacifistic). Christianity transcended political or national boundaries. It was a spiritual force intended to influence all human civilization. It grew through non-violent, yet aggressive and forceful evangelism.

Humans, whosoever, were invited to voluntarily become part of the kingdom of heaven through spiritual conversion and regeneration. Christ's kingdom on earth began in the heart. It was to transform individuals from the inside out. The Christian gospel begins with 'salvation' as the Apostle Paul, a Pharisee (Orthodox Jew), summarized to the Corinthians, 'By this gospel you are saved...'

> *For what I received I passed on to you as of first importance: that Christ died for our sins according to the Scriptures, that he was buried, that he was raised on the third day according to the Scriptures, (1 Corinthians 15:3-4).*

By 'first importance' Paul is inferring that there is something more than 'getting saved'. Spiritual 'birth' was just that, a pathway to a full spiritual life. At the highest level, the Christian gospel is not only an invitation to 'go to heaven' and 'live forever' (as is commonly understood today), but in fact, it is a call to become a new species—to become one with God, through his Son; to become an intimate and vital member of the divine family.

Just as the divine Word, the pre-incarnate Jesus, took on flesh forever, flesh (some humans) will be born (born-again, or 'adopted') into divinity.

> *But as many as received him, to them gave he power to become the sons of God, even to them that believe on his name: (John 1:12 KJV)*

This idea of 'adoption' into the family of God carries with it the responsibility of leadership or rulership. The problem of the world today is self-serving rulership. Bible prophecy tells us that is about to change.

The Christian life is a call to deny oneself; at times, to even deny the good things of earth. A true disciple is a flesh and blood member of humanity while being an operative of divinity. This self-denying rulership of the new *Adam* is what the world desperately needs and will experience sooner than later. Jesus prays for this group, his people, who would separate from the world in order to serve the world.

> *I have given them your word and the world has hated them, for they are not of the world any more than I am of the world. My prayer is not that you take them out of the world but that you protect them from the evil one. They are not of the world, even as I am not of it. (John 17:14-16)*

The prophetic ministry of *Elijah* and ultimately *Adam* will bring a new world-order called *Restoration*. *Restoration* is the larger and fuller context of salvation, and the sons of God are the agents of *Restoration*.

Human governance, i.e., humans governing humans is a Biblical concept. The problem in human history has been finding governance that is serving, not self-serving. Imagine living in a world where our government officials truly served for the benefit of the people. That hope will soon be a reality. This is the 'good news' that is coming.

In Jesus' world, ruling is sacrificial. Jesus defines his concept of ruling:

> *"And whoever desires to be first among you, let him be your slave-- "just as the Son of Man did not come to be served, but to serve, and to give His life a ransom for many." (Matthew 20:27-28)*

The 'good news' Review

And Christians, those truly 'in Christ', HAVE BEEN serving the world. Through many twists and turns, a very imperfect Christianity has 'conquered the world' with sacrificial love and truth. By 'conquered' here, we mean that Christianity, starting with a few men 2000 years ago, has become the largest and most influential religion on earth. And while it was not called to become a typical nation, its core ideals have become foundational to its larger political society. These Judeo-Christian values have become the vital bedrock of Western Civilization, the most free, humane, and prosperous civilization on earth.

Having a divine identity, ideally, Christianity is called to be an earthly expression of a loving heavenly family (Father, Holy Spirit, and Son) reconciling their human 'household' back to their Father in heaven, AND the original goodness intended for the universe. Each member of the Godhead participates in this enterprise in their unique way.

The Christian message or gospel is to the 'poor' of earth—the humble in spirit. Let's review some of the classic ideals and characteristics of those who will lead or rule in the process of *Restoration*. Here is Jesus quoting Isaiah 61 as it is a fulfilled in his life.

> *"The Spirit of the Lord is on me, because he has anointed me to preach good news to the poor. He has sent me to proclaim freedom for the prisoners and recovery of sight for the blind, to release the oppressed, to proclaim the year of the Lord's favor." (Luke 4:18-19)*

And Jesus' mission has become his disciples' mission. Those who 'believe on the Son' become part of divine leadership's mission to reconcile the earth to God. Judaism's original call to be a 'light to the gentiles' has temporarily been re-appropriated in the Christian message. In Jesus' day that message was largely expressed like this:

> *Jesus went throughout Galilee, teaching in their synagogues, preaching the good news of the kingdom, and healing every disease and sickness among the people. (Mathew 4:23)*

This exceptional moment, the unchecked demonstration of divine truth and power has not been seen since apostolic days. Nevertheless, the good news spread far and wide with the empowering witness of transformed lives. But the early demonstration of unlimited power would have to wait for another day. Meanwhile, a more indigenous witness would spread around the world.

The Christian Mandate

The New Testament is an account of the early works, theology, and instructions to the church, the servants of the Lord. The apostles would travel to distant cites starting believing communities and then, fortunately for us as well, write letters of encouragement and instruction. Let's listen in as the Apostle Peter instructs his flock on how to be lights in their own cities (Selected passages from 1 Peter chapters 1-4).

> *1:1) Peter, an apostle of Jesus Christ, To God's elect, strangers in the world,... 5who through faith are shielded by God's power until the coming of the salvation that is ready to be revealed in the last time. 6In this you greatly rejoice, though now for a little while you may have had to suffer grief in all kinds of trials. 7These have come so that your faith—of greater worth than gold, which perishes even though refined by fire--may be proved genuine and may result in praise, glory and honor when Jesus Christ is revealed. 8Though you have not seen him, you love him; and even though you do not see him now, you believe in him and are filled with an inexpressible and glorious joy,... 14As obedient children, do not conform to the evil desires you had when you lived in ignorance. 15But just as he who called you is holy, so be holy in all you do;... 17Since you call on a Father who judges each man's work impartially, live your lives as strangers here in reverent fear. 18For you know that it was not with perishable things such as silver or gold that you were redeemed from the empty way of life handed down to you from your forefathers,... 22Now that you have purified yourselves by obeying the truth so that you have sincere love for your brothers, love one another deeply, from the heart. 23For you have been born again, not of perishable seed, but of imperishable, through the living and*

*enduring word of God. ... **2:11)** Dear friends, I urge you, as aliens and strangers in the world, to abstain from sinful desires, which war against your soul. 12Live such good lives among the pagans that, though they accuse you of doing wrong, they may see your good deeds and glorify God on the day he visits us. 13Submit yourselves for the Lord's sake to every authority instituted among men: whether to the king, as the supreme authority, 14or to governors, who are sent by him to punish those who do wrong and to commend those who do right. 15For it is God's will that by doing good you should silence the ignorant talk of foolish men. ... 21To this you were called, because Christ suffered for you, leaving you an example, that you should follow in his steps. 22"He committed no sin, and no deceit was found in his mouth."... **3:17)** It is better, if it is God's will, to suffer for doing good than for doing evil. ... **4:12)** Dear friends, do not be surprised at the painful trial you are suffering, as though something strange were happening to you. 13But rejoice that you participate in the sufferings of Christ, so that you may be overjoyed when his glory is revealed. ... 17For it is time for judgment to begin with the family of God; and if it begins with us, what will the outcome be for those who do not obey the gospel of God?*

A tested faith; doing good—so the world may see your good deeds and glorify God. Peter's insightful instructions would become the playbook of the Christian journey for 2000 years. Even facing great opposition and suffering while penetrating pagan darkness, the Christian witness would succeed, generally, without the sword, and often nourished by the blood of the saints.

Christian Persecution

The Christian life is validated by suffering rather than conquest. Victory and rulership is through the agency of suffering. We have our examples. Chiefly, with the innocent blood of our Lord, and the apostolic 'fathers'. According to tradition, of the twelve and Paul only John may have died a natural death, the rest martyred, many cruelly.

[And according to tradition, John survived only after being thrown into boiling oil at Rome.] [For further information on the subject of Christian persecution look up Wikipedia's "Persecution of Christians" from the first century (50 screen pages), and "Persecution of Christians in the modern era", persecution of Christians since 1989, (another 13 pages)]

An online Newsweek article dated 1/4/2018 by Cristina Maza begins like this:

The persecution and genocide of Christians across the world is worse today "than at any time in history," and Western governments are failing to stop it, a report from a Catholic organization said.

The study by 'Aid to the Church in Need' [A report on Christians oppressed for their faith 2015-2017] said the treatment of Christians has worsened substantially in the past two years compared with the two years prior, and has grown more violent than any other period in modern times.

"Not only are Christians more persecuted than any other faith group, but ever-increasing numbers are experiencing the very worst forms of persecution," the report said.

Another website, 'The Esther Project' (theestherproject.com), a voice for the persecuted Church worldwide, has gathered the statistics:

Historical Christian Persecution Statistics

- More than 70 million Christians have been martyred in the course of history. More than half were martyred in the 20th century under communist and fascist government (Gordon-Conwell Resources).
- In the 21st century, roughly 100,000 to 160,000 Christians were killed each year (Gordon-Conwell Resources and World Christian Database, respectively).

- Roughly 1,093,000 Christians were martyred, worldwide, between 2000 and 2010 (World Christian Database).

Modern, Global Church Persecution Statistics - Each month...

- 322 Christians are killed for their faith (Open Doors).
- 214 churches and Christian properties are destroyed (Open Doors).
- 772 forms of violence (beatings, kidnappings, rape, arrest, etc.) are committed against Christians (Open Doors).

Heroes of Faith

So many heroes of faith! Yet, persecution of faith did not begin with Christians. Faith in God transcends Testaments and cultures. The writer of Hebrews gives us a similar faith report, the 'faith chapter', Chapter 11.

11:1Now faith is being sure of what we hope for and certain of what we do not see. 2This is what the ancients were commended for. 3By faith we understand..., 4By faith Abel... 5By faith Enoch... 6And without faith it is impossible to please God, because anyone who comes to him must believe that he exists and that he rewards those who earnestly seek him. 7By faith Noah... 8By faith Abraham... 13All these people were still living by faith when they died. They did not receive the things promised; they only saw them and welcomed them from a distance. And they admitted that they were aliens and strangers on earth.... 20By faith Isaac... Jacob..., Joseph..., Moses..., 33who through faith conquered kingdoms, administered justice... 35Women received back their dead, raised to life again. Others were tortured and refused to be released, so that they might gain a better resurrection. 36Some faced jeers and flogging, while still others were chained and put in prison. 37They were stoned; they were sawed in two; they were put to death by the sword. They went about in sheepskins and goatskins, destitute, persecuted and mistreated--38the world was not worthy of them. They

> *wandered in deserts and mountains, and in caves and holes in the ground.*

And notice this remarkable ending...

> *39These were all commended for their faith, yet none of them received what had been promised. 40God had planned something better for us so that only together with us would they be made perfect.*

Being Made Perfect

'*The world was not worthy of them*'. This cloud of witnesses did not receive the things promised; they only saw them and welcomed them from a distance. What are those things promised? What 'joy' did the ancients foresee in faith that made them 'endure their cross'? The text tells us they were part of a strategic process it refers to as '**being made perfect**'.

This fascinating subject of 'perfection' is quite complex and poorly understood, so we'll have to leave a longer detailed discussion for later. But having 'perfection' as an end-goal was empowering for the ancients, and is even more vital for us today.

In the typical Christian mindset heaven is the goal. While heaven has been quite an effective motivation for a pagan world, it is quite deficient as an incentive to an adult world. The writer of Hebrews points to an end-goal much more correct and comprehensive—perfection.

Perfection is not a place (heaven), it is a nature. Perfection is the fulness of one's identity. If salvation is spiritual birth, perfection is becoming a man, full stature. Perfection is both a process and an achievement. It has individual, corporate, and universal dimensions.

Perfection is a package deal. It is generally the subject we have been discussing in this book we call, *Restoration*. It is a new world-order via the conquest of sin, and the effects of sin. It is absolute conquest over the sin nature in perfect obedience; a legal return to the right to rule as an 'adult'. This is what the ancients welcomed from a distance.

And one last critical point: perfection in our context is pre-resurrection. Earned-earthly-perfection (perfect obedience to God within the framework of the law of Moses) was an essential element of Jesus' nature and ministry. He was the unblemished (perfect) Lamb of God.

Likewise, perfection, is also a vital achievement in the nature and identity of humanity (specifically the RULERS), **before resurrection**.

Christian Perfection

For those 'in-Christ', perfection, or more technically correct, prophetic-sinless-perfection, is full conformity to his likeness and the purposes of God. This is the same objective that Jesus points to in his first sermon, the Sermon on the Mount, when he directs his own to '**be perfect**' (Mathew 5:48). The cross of Christ purchased, above all else, perfection. Perfection is the end-target of our faith, not regeneration (justification, personal salvation). Personal regeneration alone will never set creation free from the effects of sin, only perfection will. Both regeneration and perfection are 'graces' provided by the work of Christ.

> *Let us fix our eyes on Jesus, the author and perfecter of our faith, who for the joy set before him endured the cross, scorning its shame, and sat down at the right hand of the throne of God. (Hebrews 12:2)*

We are using the word perfect here in our study quoting from the Book of Hebrews. Some form of that word is used more than twelve times in Hebrews. It's ironic that Christianity has named the book 'Hebrews' when the word 'Hebrew' or 'Jew' doesn't appear in the book. A much more fitting name for the Book of Hebrews would be the Book of Perfection.

The typical Christian has little knowledge of perfection in spite of the fact it has early roots in the Christian faith. Wikipedia makes this statement in its article, "Christian Perfection"

> *"The roots of the doctrine of Christian perfection lie in the writings of the early Church Fathers, chiefly Irenaeus, Clement of Alexandria, Origen and later Macarius of Egypt and Gregory of Nyssa."*

Perfection is such a broad and complex subject it is often referred to with different words or terms both theologically as well as Biblically.

Eastern Christian theology used the term Theosis or Deification, while Western/Catholic Christian theology used the term Divinization. Protestant tradition generally (overemphasizing 'faith alone') rejected any perfection theology with the exception of Methodists/Wesleyans (John Wesley). Modern thinkers such as C. S. Lewis integrated perfection themes into much of his writing. Of course, there was/is wide variation (and even mischaracterization) of what perfection is and how it manifests itself in practice.

The Bible also uses different terms for perfection. One interesting example is the Book of Revelation. The Father ends each review of the seven churches with a perfection formula, *"To him who overcomes"*, adding to one of them, *"and does my will to the end"*. These are intimate/individual promises given to the Body corporately (for instance: "to rule over the nations…with an iron scepter…"). These are examples of 'full conformity': a 'bride without spot', a 'spiritual temple', etc. Below is a short review of the 'overcomes' verses:

To him who overcomes (and does my will to the end) …

- I will give the right to eat from the tree of life, which is in the paradise of God. (Rev 2:7)
- will not be hurt at all by the second death. (Rev 2:11)

- I will give some of the hidden manna. I will also give him a white stone with a new name written on it, known only to him who receives it. (Rev 2:17)
- I will give authority over the nations-- 'He will rule them with an iron scepter; he will dash them to pieces like pottery' (Rev 2:26)
- will be dressed in white. I will never blot out his name from the book of life, but will acknowledge his name before my Father and his angels. (Rev 3:5)
- I will make a pillar in the temple of my God. Never again will he leave it. I will write on him the name of my God and the name of the city of my God, the new Jerusalem, which is coming down out of heaven from my God; and I will also write on him my new name. (Rev 3:12)
- I will give the right to sit with me on my throne, just as I overcame and sat down with my Father on his throne. (Rev 3:21)
- will inherit all this, and I will be his God and he will be my son. (Rev 21:7)

Yes, honest-to-goodness perfection, whether it is called overcoming, victory, freedom, restoration, a harvest of righteousness, a glorious church without spot or wrinkle, or anything else, is the untold story in todays' Christian theology. It was a driving force for the ancients. One wonders if perfection is a motivating end-goal for Christians today? How about you, the reader?

Perfection is seldom mentioned and often disparaged. Perfection ultimately validates the efficacy of God's work of grace in mankind. Perfection is the core objective of the *Restoration*, and true faith is the soil in which it has grown and will finally bloom.

Whereby are given unto us exceeding great and precious promises: that by these ye might be partakers of the divine nature, having escaped the corruption that is in the world through lust. (2 Peter 1:4 KJV)

'All have sinned' is a bitter and constant reality for mankind. But, the Word of God promised the ancients, and us, something better—not just atonement (the covering of sin) but freedom (the absence of sinning). The ability to see and live life beyond the material / visible realm is a quality essential for godly, eternal life. Each faithful generation has been tested with light, with promises, and with objectives they were given. Each built upon a foundation previously laid, and the baton is passed to the next generation. Many have pleased God along the journey. In terms of faith, it is a single and successful story with many acts.

Faith is where it starts. Faith is the first division of humanity. This ancient war between faith and faithlessness, is still in our headlines, and even more troubling, in our churches, disguised in many forms. But the process of refinement and growth is working, and right on schedule.

> *...for everyone born of God overcomes the world. This is the victory that has overcome the world, even our faith. (1 John 5:4)*
>
> *No one who is born of God will continue to sin, because God's seed remains in him; he cannot go on sinning, because he has been born of God. (1 John 3:9)*

It is vital for us, just like the ancients, to see and welcome this proper end-goal. Today, perfection is no longer distant; the essential script (the gospel-of-the-kingdom) and the stage (Israel / Jerusalem) are in place to begin that final journey. One simply cannot understand the next prophetic age without this foundation.

A New Portfolio

In light of what is coming next, it is important to have this story of the story vivid in our thinking. Through both Testaments (Old and New), God has given the world a testimony of the 'lambs'. Even now, the light is continuing to be revealed to the world by the 'word of their testimony', and 'they loved not their lives unto death'.

These outcasts who have faithfully given of themselves in service to God are about to be given a new portfolio. The 'suffering servants', following in their Lord's footsteps in giving of their lives, are about to take on a new prophetic role—'conquering king'.

This is a radically new role for Christian ministry. It may appear contradictory to our current meek and gentle ministry style.

> *Behold, I send you forth as sheep in the midst of wolves: be ye therefore wise as serpents, and harmless as doves. (Mathew 10:16 KJV)*

Officially, the gospel must be presented with love, and received voluntarily. Being a strong influence, yes, but the idea of directly imposing the will of God on human society is antithetical to most Christian traditions. The idea of moving from a voluntary spiritual-order to a dictating-order might seem quite inappropriate to many. Spiritual authority dictating to secular authority is in violation of the Western truism, 'separation of church and state'. But that must soon change.

Up until now (for 2000 years) Christianity has rightly emphasized the ministry of voluntary, personal regeneration, we call being 'saved' or 'born-again'. But we have to analyze that 'salvation' idea a little closer. Without spiting hairs, that ministry promotes an extra-world or out-of-this-world identity. We have quoted some of those passages earlier:

> *Peter in 1 Peter 1: To God's elect, <u>strangers in the world</u>; Jesus in John 17: for they are <u>not of the world</u> any more than I am of the world.*

This 'heavenly' (not of this world) emphasis has ultimately brought us into a place of conflict with the full gospel. God's intent is the restoration of both heaven and earth. A ministry calling for humans to voluntarily leave their earthly citizenship in favor of heavenly citizenship leaves half of our ministry undone. Remember the opening of the Lord's Prayer, *thy will be done on earth as it is in heaven*.

And it's important to note: the 'God's will on earth' part, <u>cannot be accomplished fully on a voluntary basis</u>. 'Earthly salvation' cannot be accomplished with a 'heavenly salvation' ministry (today's evangelism). Earthly salvation will eventually require coercion or force. Righteous (lamb) 'kings' will have to take their rightful place and forcefully bring order. That is the little understood story of prophecy. Notice, according to prophecy, Jesus, the Lamb of God, will also play this dual role. The 'lamb' ministry is not enough:

> *They will make war against the Lamb, but the Lamb <u>will overcome them</u> because he is Lord of lords and King of kings-- and with him will be his called, chosen and faithful followers."*
> *(Revelation 17:14)*

Ruling on earth, before the resurrection, is not part of Christianity's mindset, but it is part of prophecy, rightly understood. Christ's followers, who are 'lambs' by nature, are kings by identity. Christ is called the King of kings`.

The subject of this book, *Restoration*, is a kingly ministry, or royal priesthood. The key players *Adam*, *Elijah*, and *Joseph* (explained elsewhere in this book) are prophetic kings. Each have RULER-ship roles in the *Restoration*.

Both suffering and ruling are the two legitimate and essential dimensions of the Messianic ministry, the ministries of Messiah and his followers. Kingdom rulers are formed through suffering. Or perhaps we should say, perfection (or near perfection), produced by suffering, forms kingdom rulers. Only those exemplifying the life of Christ, in fact, members of Christ, are qualified to rule (in a universal sense).

It is well known that Messiah comes to rule; to defeat and dismiss the satanic and human forces allied against him and his kingdom. We see this picture clearly in the book of Revelation. But the Christian church directly taking on this role, pre-resurrection, is virtually unknown.

Forceful Reordering

But the framework for this new ministry is quite simple, drawing on the context we are given from the Garden of Eden. Two immutable forces are contending with each other, God and Satan. This warfare is played out through man... Man stumbled! Man diminished himself and his creation. Only man can lift himself and his creation back to its full potential and standing, using the gracious legal framework God will provide.

God provides a (costly and legal) way, but man, representing God, must struggle through to the final victory. And in a sense, there is only one measure of victory—man restoring himself to PERFECTION. All the rest of creation will reflect his perfection. That is the short story.

> *His intent was that now, through the church, the manifold wisdom of God should be made known to the rulers and authorities in the heavenly realms, (Ephesians 3:10)*

In other sections of this book we have attempted to explain HOW that victory is achieved through the generation-long process of *Restoration*.

In closing this section, let's just briefly review the Scriptural thread that runs through the Bible defining the agents (RULERS) of *Restoration*. Here is the first mention of the nature of the conflict and the solution:

> *And I will put enmity between you and the woman, and between your offspring and hers; he will crush your head, and you will strike his heel." (Genesis 3:15)*

Eve's offspring, the King and kings (RULERS), will crush Satan's head. This defeat comes in two steps, both dealt by man, for it is only man who can defeat Satan. First, the Son of Man has come to legally defeat Satan (de jure victory) and provide the context for the eventual defeat (de facto victory) of Satan. In Romans, Paul clarifies who the conquering (de facto victory) group of mankind will be:

> *The God of peace will soon crush Satan <u>under your feet</u>. (Romans 16:20a)*

Under 'your feet'! The church, the sons of God, is the group who will crush Satan.

To conquer Satan today, he must be rooted out of humanity and human society. That cannot be understood apart from the three people groups that we are discussing in this section.

Today, the wheat and tares, the wise and the foolish, grow together, at times virtually indistinguishable from each other. There must be a process of separation and clarification. And there must be someone to wisely manage that process.

That prophetic wisdom is found in the sons of God. These RULERS are themselves being finally conformed to the Son even as they manage the larger process of rooting Satan out of the governments of earth.

Forcefully reordering and restoring righteousness to the people and nations of earth is the responsibility of the RULERS. This re-creation of the earth is not by military or nuclear might, but by unlimited supernatural spiritual power. This power can only be given to, and managed by, the RULERS (after an internal reordering mentioned in Chapter 4: A NEW PROPHETIC ORDER).

We see the authority and the power to crush the nations in one of the 'overcoming' verses quoted above:

> *I will give authority over the nations-- 'He will rule them with an iron scepter; he will dash them to pieces like pottery' (Rev 2:26)*

Here, 'dash them to pieces' is the same word used for 'crushed' in the Romans 16:20 verse above. Satan is crushed when his access to pliant men is diminished through a heightened presence of God, and the implementation of new righteous government.

Specifically, this re-creation process is directed by *Elijah* the prophet, the prophetic ministry of the RULERS. *Elijah* (and company) is the 'voice' of testimony to the nations Jesus refers to in Mathew 24:14 as the gospel-of-the-kingdom. We discussed this ministry of *Elijah* in greater detail toward the end of 'Chapter 8: HOW IT ALL BEGINS— HUMAN INITIATIVE. *Elijah* is the 'Exodus' prophet who dictates new 'kingdom terms' to the world. Both Deuteronomy 18:19 and Acts 3:22 give a warning concerning this prophet (effectively saying to the world, including the Christian world), '*you must listen to everything he tells you.*'

The whole world for the first time will see God clearly; they will know that '*he exists and that he rewards those who earnestly seek him*'. A final testimony will be given and the 'end' will come. *Elijah* will then go on to dictate to a crushed world the foundations of a new world order.

As noted in Chapter 9: BUILDING A BORN-AGAIN WORLD (The End of the World): Christianity successfully 'wins' (or conquers) the world. In fact, each Millennium commission in Mathew 24 has the element of 'conquest' in it. Christianity conquers finally, not with evangelism, but with prophetic wisdom and power (beginning with the 'gospel-of-the-kingdom' and the Last Passover, etc.).

This is the 'end' of the world as we know it, but it's also the end of evangelical Christianity. The Sons of God are now revealed. The 'go to heaven gospel' (the right to become a son of God) is now over. That privilege has ended at the revealing of the Sons. The world, the people of the world, will now need a new gospel, a new spiritual end-goal and a new model of righteousness, which is effectively the lifestyle lived by Jesus and the apostles—Torah Judaism.

In the *Elijah* conquest, the Sons of God have not been perfected yet, but they have begun that journey separate from the world. These sons, effectively adopted into the family of God, will become 'rulers', prophetic overseers (with Messiah), of God's eternal universal kingdom. That is their identity—eternally. They will eventually have unique qualities such as glorified immortal bodies, will not reproduce, and become part of the divine family. These RULERS are citizens of heaven who as a mystical body, paradoxically, have both a 'male' and 'female' ministry or function. Some of those functions are expressed Biblically as the Sons of God (kings), the Bride of Christ, and the Spiritual Temple. In our discussions here, we will refer to them as RULERS or sons of God. They are called to *'prepare the way'* for the King.

Incidentally, the Apostolic fathers named themselves 'the Way', not 'Christians'. One can see how clearly they saw their mission to 'prepare the way' for the reign of the King.

CITIZENS

So now we have the kingdom's King (Messiah) and Body (RULERS), but every kingdom must have 'citizens'. In the larger context of the universal kingdom of God, the people of earth are the citizens.

These citizens (CITIZENS) of the kingdom, are the missing people group in Christian theology. In a sense they are the native 'rulers' of earth, overseen by the universal rulers.

Their unique qualities are eternal flesh and blood mortal bodies; they will marry and reproduce and be self-governing within their own jurisdiction. They will be the eternal natives of earth, and probably other 'earths' (in the universe), eventually.

Of the increase of his government and peace there will be no end. (Isaiah 9:7)

Notable among these 'citizens', is natural Israel, the Royal House of David, the first nation of earth. It will dwell peacefully and prosperously within its promised, much enlarged, Biblical boundaries with its reestablished Levitical priesthood being a light to the rest of the world.

Adam and Eve prefigure this earth-citizen type. If they had not fallen, they would have lived forever (eating of the Tree of Life) as citizens of earth, enjoying the bountiful goodness of earth. Adam was made of earth; (we can presume) his highest aspirations were to live forever in Paradise. Frankly, for most people, the pleasures of earth are what they want, and more than they can handle. Heaven, for most people, is just a place that has all their favorite earthly pleasures in abundance.

REBELS

All of general humanity will be separated into three groups. Tragically (from a human perspective), one of the groups, the rebels, will be eliminated from the living universe. According to the Book of Revelation (Chapters 20 and 21) they, along with the fallen angels, will be cast into the lake of fire, experiencing what is called 'the second death'. A telling feature of this group is their lack of faith.

Although the three groups may not be divided equally (into thirds), it is interesting to note the number of 'third' judgements in Revelation, including a likely reference to a third part of rebel angels cast out of heaven and a third part of men dying:

And his tail drew the third part of the stars of heaven, and did cast them to the earth: and the dragon stood before the woman which was ready to be delivered, for to devour her child as soon as it was born. (Rev. 12:4 KJV)

...the third part of trees was burnt up, (Rev. 8:7 KJV)

...the third part of the sea became blood; (Rev. 8:8 KJV)

And the <u>third part</u> of the creatures which were in the sea, and had life, died; and the third part of the ships were destroyed. (Rev. 8:9 KJV)

...and there fell a great star from heaven, burning as it were a lamp, and it fell upon the <u>third part</u> of the rivers, and upon the fountains of waters; (Rev. 8:10 KJV)

...and the <u>third part</u> of the waters became wormwood; and many men died of the waters, because they were made bitter (Rev 8:11 KJV)

...and the <u>third part</u> of the sun was smitten, and the <u>third part</u> of the moon, and the <u>third part</u> of the stars; so as the <u>third part</u> of them was darkened, and the day shone not for a <u>third part</u> of it, and the night likewise. (Rev. 8:12 KJV)

By these three was the <u>third part</u> of men killed... (Rev, 9:18 KJV)

So, we see the existence of a third people group, rebels, who will eventually be eliminated from the living universe.

The two-people-groups theology of heaven (RULERS) and hell (REBELS) is well known within Christianity. It is the existence of the third group, the 'citizen' (earthly) group that needs our attention to rightly understand the *Restoration*. How has this group been so invisible to Biblical scholarship, even when in plain sight? Perhaps there is no greater testimony to this truth of invisibility then this verse:

It is the glory of God to conceal a matter; to search out a matter is the glory of kings. (Proverbs 25:2)

Now, let's review some important distinctions found within the three people groups.

Faith and Roles

To picture the three groups in faith terms, we start with every human who has ever lived. Some of these humans had/have faith and some did/do not. Humans without faith are essentially part of the REBELS group; humans with faith alone are CITIZENS; and humans with faith and blood (the redemptive blood of Jesus) are RULERS.

With this understanding, we begin to have greater prophetic insight into many of the events recorded in Scripture, and why the end-of-the-age *Restoration* has to account for all three people groups.

The groups are identified in this fashion. Initially the RULERS are revealed as the Sons of God (to reset the world). After being revealed, this group is essentially 'closed'.

Over an extended period, a new generation (of each group) grow up fully aware of the truth and the reality of the God of Israel. With full knowledge of God and his righteousness, the remaining humans will migrate spiritually toward one of the two 'open' groups. The end of the *Restoration* period sees the first division of CITIZENS and REBELS when the Messiah returns (Sheep and Goats).

The roles are divided like this: the RULERS (heavenly people) are a prophetic priesthood who manage, oversee, and judge. The CITIZENS (earthly people) enter their role as the native population and authority on earth. And the REBELS try to thwart it all, even as a chaotic world is transformed into a kingdom world. This is a short description of the complex events required of the first generation of the kingdom (Millennium).

Why have we missed such a critical process BEFORE the return of Messiah? Why haven't we seen evidence of two (not one) living eternal people groups? [Note: In a sense, the rebels are also an eternal group, but eternally damned. When we use the term 'eternal' we mean 'eternally living'. The Bible says the REBELS experience the 'second death', which infers a state of 'eternal death' even while existing eternally.]

Apparently, in God's sovereign plan, three-people-groups would have been distracting before its time. But after carefully evaluating the evidence, will we continue to deny this truth?

The REBELS group and their activities have been given far too much prophetic press. The real breakthrough in prophetic literacy comes from understanding the two 'positive' people groups. Let's continue with a brief survey the theological and Scriptural arguments that support the idea of two 'good' people groups. Again, the principle of the two groups begins back in Genesis.

Holiness

Perhaps the most pervasive concept in the universe, first stated in Genesis 2:3, is holiness. Most Christians need a refresher course in holiness. As early Christianity separated itself from Judaism (which makes Biblical holiness a high priority), they began to modify the concept of holiness. Similar to the issue of heaven and hell, holiness was transformed into an issue of good and evil. Holiness was effectively redefined as a separation from evil.

But that is not the primary tenet of holiness. Holiness is the separation or dividing of that which is good. In the first two chapters of Genesis, in which everything is good, we get at least three holiness examples, one named as such. Heaven (holy) is set apart from earth. The seventh day (holy) is set apart from six days. And Eve (holy) is set apart from Adam. As recorded, evil is non-existent in the universe at this point. Holiness, in its primary state, is defined totally apart from evil.

Holy is the product of dividing something good into two parts. One of the parts is called holy, and the other part is often called common. Maintaining holiness, is properly maintaining the separation of two good parts.

This applies to humans as well. If there is to be a holy people, there needs to be a common people, and both the holy and the common are 'good'. Think about it. By definition, the Christian definition of holy, as applied to humans ('saints' and 'aints'), is impossible.

The term 'saints' (holy ones) is used nearly one hundred times throughout the Old and New Testaments. Holy people, places, and things may also be separated from evil things, but by definition, holy is maintaining the separation of two good thing. Un-holy in an unblemished universe would simply mean 'common'. But in the confusion of our present corrupt world, un-holy could, and does, mean both common or evil. Therefore, we must to be alert to the difference.

There are seven 'good' days of the week, but God and man sanctify the Sabbath by maintaining distinct rules that separate the seventh day from the other six. Technically, holy is the separation of two GOOD things, not the separation of good from evil.

Stars and Sands

Abraham is the 'trunk' of the faith tree. He connects all who have faith to divine roots. The Book of Romans (4:11) says Abraham is the father of all who believe (all who have faith, circumcised and uncircumcised). He is the father of 'many nations' (two types of nations, 4:18). He is the father of us all (4:16). Then after he had been tested with Isaac, he gets this blessing from God:

> *That in blessing I will bless thee, and in multiplying I will multiply thy seed as the <u>stars of the heaven</u>, and as the <u>sand which [is] upon the sea shore</u>; and thy seed shall possess the gate of his enemies... (Genesis 22:17 KJV)*

At first reading, this blessing appears to be directly addressing the 'quantity' of Abraham's faithful descendants. But the way it is phrased hints of something much deeper. This picture of the stars and the sands is continuing the theme of two eternal jurisdictions revealed in the first verse of the Bible – heaven and earth.

The stars and sands give us a beautiful representation of the two distinct multitudes of faithful humans running through sacred history. But notice also the third group represented in this Scripture—the enemies (REBELS), those dispossessed of any earthly or material inheritance, '*thy seed shall possess the gate of his enemies...*' This Scripture is the Bible's first concise mention of the 'three people groups'.

Abraham had two blessed sons both having twelve sons (tribes). The symbolism is clear, Abraham's two sons represent the fullness of God's good purposes for heaven and earth.

Two Mothers, Two Sons, Two Births

The New Testament adds to this narrative. In Galatians 4, Paul explains essential characteristics of each son and mother. One was a 'slave' and one was 'free'. Paul puts a more formal framework around the two sons and the two mothers. The mothers now represent two covenants.

> *For it is written that Abraham had two sons, one by the slave woman and the other by the free woman. His son by the slave woman was born according to the flesh, but his son by the free woman was born as the result of a divine promise. These things are being taken figuratively: The women represent two covenants. One covenant is from Mount Sinai and bears children who are to be slaves: This is Hagar. Now Hagar stands for Mount Sinai in Arabia and corresponds to the present city of Jerusalem, because she is in slavery with her children. But the Jerusalem that is above is free, and she is our mother. (Galatians 4:22-26 NIV)*

This is very tricky theology and almost always misunderstood. Putting aside the issue of law verses grace, which is the local issue here, Paul appeals to the prophetic (big picture) to buttress his argument. Prophetically, Paul is reaffirming two 'faithful' people groups. One birth represents a 'birth according to the flesh', and one birth represents a 'birth according to the spirit'. One covenant is represented by 'Mount Sinai in Arabia' (earthly) and one is represented by the 'Jerusalem that is above' (heavenly).

The slave and free terminology here is just a metaphorical aid comparing the relative natures of earthly, fleshly people (CITIZENS) verses heavenly, spiritual people (RULERS). Those terms DO NOT represent evil versus good. Pause a moment and ponder this before you move on. It is so important that it deserves some extra time and consideration. Slave and free terminology DOES NOT represent evil versus good!

Two Covenants

Regarding the two covenants in Paul's debate, when we sort it all out, we see that there are two distinct identity covenants. One began at Mt. Sinai when Moses read the Book of the Covenant and the people said 'I do'. Doesn't this sound like one of our sacred sacraments?

> *Then he took the Book of the Covenant and read it to the people. They responded, "We will do everything the LORD has said; we will obey." Moses then took the blood, sprinkled it on the people and said, "This is the blood of the covenant that the LORD has made with you in accordance with all these words." (Exodus 24:7-8)*

It was sealed with 'blood of the covenant' sprinkled on the people. Roughly 1500 years later, Jesus would come preaching the 'kingdom of heaven' to a people who were looking for the 'kingdom of earth' (the Royal House of David). He would call out disciples who he would teach, empower, and send into the whole world preaching the gospel-of-the-kingdom (which quickly became reduced to the gospel of salvation).

At Passover, on his last night before he was crucified, he gave his magnum opus (John 14-17), a grand marriage proposal telling his disciples (present and future) they would (someday) be CONFORMED TO HIS LIKENESS and DO EVEN GREATER WORKS than he. As he ate his last meal with his disciples, he sealed this covenant. He asked them to do something anathema to Judaism—to eat his body and drink his blood.

> *This is my blood of the covenant, which is poured out for many for the forgiveness of sins. (Matthew 26:28 NIV)*

With this sacrament, he was declaring his disciple's (future and past followers) eternal identity (as RULERS) and a mystical union with him. He was reaffirming the blood covenant offered on Sinai.

There is still great confusion about this. The blood, marriage covenant given on Sinai, and reaffirmed by Jesus at the Last Supper, is actually represented by the '*Jerusalem that is above*', a free covenant. There is a covenant that is NOT a blood, marriage covenant—the Jerimiah 31 NEW COVENANT. It is the lesser, slave covenant, represented by '*the present city of Jerusalem*', pointed to by Paul in Galatians mentioned above. Again, take a moment to ponder this. It is of paramount importance.

Here we see God has made provision, in Abraham's two sons, two mothers, and two births for two identity covenants for two eternal people groups. One group (earthy) saved by faith and one (heavenly) saved by faith and blood. To illustrate that even more clearly, we can look at lessons from the Exodus (Passover).

Redemption and Freedom

Christians rightly point to the saving blood of Jesus who was, in effect, the (Passover) Lamb who takes away the sin of the world. Christian redemption is in the substitutionary blood of Jesus. But, going back to the original account of Exodus, if we look closely, we can recognize a fascinating nuance.

The Passover was conducted by family groups or multiple family groups depending on the number of people and the size of the lamb. The lamb was killed and its blood applied to the doorpost of the home. This is the proto-pattern for Jesus' blood sacrifice.

It has been widely assumed that as the death-angel swept across Egypt, the blood 'saved' everyone inside the home. But if we stop and think for a moment, we should realize that this is not true.

It was only the firstborns (males) who were in danger, so only the firstborns were 'saved' by the blood. For instance, in a home with twenty people, perhaps only three or four were firstborns. All twenty were 'saved' from Egypt and bondage, but only three or four were redeemed by the blood. They all ate of the lamb, but not all were saved by the blood. Most of the people leaving Egypt were NOT saved by the blood.

In Hebrews 12:23 Jesus' church is called the 'church of the firstborn'. Here again, in this Passover sacrament, is clear evidence of two people groups, two faithful groups. They all left Egypt, they were all set free, but only a small remnant was 'saved' by the blood.

Two Priesthoods

Just as there is a covenant for each people group, there is a priesthood for each group as well. Israel's priesthood, and in the coming larger context, the earth's priesthood, are men descended from Levi and Aaron.

The Levitical priesthood is the priesthood of earth; the priesthood of the Temple economy; in it there are priests who intercede for the people of earth. It is a product of the earthly kingdom, an extension of the Royal House of David (Israel). The seventy judges of the Sanhedrin and the seventy sacrifices of the Feast of Tabernacles, in which all the nations of earth must participate, (Zech. 14:16), reflect the Biblical commission of Israel's larger priestly ministry to the nations of the world.

But there is another, almost unnoticed (especially in the OT), priestly thread that runs throughout Scripture. It is the priestly order of Melchizedek (Palms 110:4, Hebrews 5:10). We first see Melchizedek, as the king of Salem, giving bread and wine (as in communion?) to Abraham after Abraham rescued Lot (Genesis 14:18).

> *And Melchizedek king of Salem brought forth bread and wine: and he [was] the priest of the most high God. And he blessed him, and said, Blessed [be] Abram of the most high God, possessor of heaven and earth: (Genesis 14:18-19 KJV)*

This blessing, and the bread and wine, given to Abram by Melchizedek appears to be highly significant. It is immediately after this blessing that the whole Abrahamic redemptive dynasty begins.

Fortunately, the Book of Hebrews gives greater insight into this mysterious figure and event. It supports the idea of two priesthoods for two people groups by showing the contrast and role of each priesthood.

Hebrews explains that Messiah, Jesus, was also a priest, but in the 'order' of Melchizedek. Jesus was from the tribe of Judah so he could not be part of earth's Levitical priestly order (Hebrews 8:4). Instead he was part of a 'higher' (heavenly) priestly order.

Hebrews tells us that the account in Genesis 14 revealed a lesser and greater priestly hierarchy (as a priestly order) between Melchizedek and the Levitical priesthood. Melchizedek blessed the Levitical, and the Levitical paid tithes to Melchizedek.

> *This man, however, did not trace his descent from Levi, yet he collected a tenth from Abraham and blessed him who had the promises. And without doubt the lesser is blessed by the greater. (Hebrews 7:6-7)*

Hebrews affirms an eternal Levitical order, but acknowledges the limitations of it. And it also raises the question still not understood by Christianity itself:

> *If perfection could have been attained through the Levitical priesthood--and indeed the law given to the people established that priesthood--why was there still need for another priest to come, one in the order of Melchizedek, not in the order of Aaron? (Hebrews 7:11)*

How does man totally conquer sin and become perfect? The short answer is that the Levitical system could 'manage' human failure (sin), but it could not 'conquer' human failure (bring perfection).

Jesus came, a priest in the (heavenly) order of Melchizedek, to provide 'perfection' to the sons of God, who would then, themselves, enter into the order of Melchizedek, a royal (kingly) priesthood (1 Peter 2:9).

Neither of these priesthoods merge with each other, nor are subsumed by the other. Just as noted in the Book of Hebrews, the two priesthoods are both distinct and eternal. In God's eternal economy they complement each other. Both the heavenly and earthly priestly offices, like the covenants, are needed and will last forever. They personify the RULER and CITIZEN people groups.

Half-time Review

Let's review our discussion thus far about people groups. If we set aside the third EVIL/REBEL group for a moment, we can see a stream of Scriptural evidence for two 'good' people groups. From the first verse of the Bible we recognize two eternal jurisdictions—heaven and earth. Those jurisdictions, representing two people groups, are threaded throughout Scripture. Next, they are separated utilizing the concept of holiness—holy vs. common. It continues with Abraham's descendants likened to 'stars and sands'. Those descendants came from two mothers of two sons, and two types of birth. We also have two salvations—faith and faith plus blood (freedom and redemption). Then we have the critical provisions of two identity covenants, and now two identity priesthoods.

This should start to challenge our concept of a 'heaven and hell' universe. But wait, there's more! We have Israel itself being split into two houses, the House of Judah and the House of Ephraim (Joseph). We have the dreamer, Joseph, being split apart from his brothers, distinguishing the idea of RULER and CITIZENS. Also, we should not forget Christianity being split from its parent, Judaism (both have unique and valid messages). Next, we will visit what may be the quintessential treatise on three people groups—the book of Romans. Than we will return to Matthew 24-25 and Jesus' own words on people groups.

Chapter Eleven

THREE PEOPLE GROUPS IN THE BOOK OF ROMANS

The Epistle to the Romans is the most theological book of the New Testament, a masterpiece of advanced doctrine. It is often recognized as a master treatise on justification and salvation, but the greater prophetic design of Romans which specifically addresses the three people groups is largely overlooked.

In general, overlooking the three groups throughout the entire Bible is commonplace. The tendency is for, both student and scholar, to see the theological trees rather than the eschatological forest. This is partly a result of reading and interpreting Scripture with preconceived biases, such as a 'heaven and hell only' perspective. The Book of Romans is clearly designed around the idea of three people groups.

Calvary

Rightly understood, the main theological content of Romans, chapters 1-11, has a prophetic structure. (The last five chapters (12-16) generally deal with pastoral issues). Those first eleven chapters are designed around what is perhaps the best-known iconic scene in Christendom—the hill of Calvary and the three crosses. The scene is based on Scripture:

Then were there two thieves crucified with him, one on the right hand, and another on the left. (Matthew 27:38 KJV)

Why three crosses, and what do they represent in the crucifixion story? These three crosses depict the symbolic ends of all humanity. Every human who ever lived will become a member of one of these representative groups, and the rewards or punishments accordingly. The crosses depict the three people groups grounded in concepts taken from the first three chapters of Genesis—holy, common and evil.

In a sense, Romans could be thought of as Genesis II. Drawing on these foundational patterns, Paul addresses each group individually.

REBELS, RULERS and CITIZENS, Paul deals with each in turn. Like a great artist, he begins painting his canvas as the Bible does, with a black background...

"... and darkness was upon the face of the deep...." (Genesis 1:2)

REBELS

The first chapter of Romans deals with the REBELS. You will notice that my book gives very little time to evil or the workings of evil directly. This is generally a pattern followed by Scripture and Romans. We always gain more by emphasizing and understanding the positive rather than the negative. That's not to ignore evil, but to use it as a background or contrast for the good.

After some opening statements, Paul addresses the prophetic nature of evil in only fifteen verses (1:18-1:32). It is perhaps the most brilliant, insightful, and concise analysis of evil ever written. It would be worth our while to spend a few minutes analyzing it.

Slavery Verses Rebellion

Paul begins with this verse:

The wrath of God is being revealed from heaven against all the godlessness and wickedness of men who suppress the truth by their wickedness... (1:18)

Notice the phrase: *"suppress the truth by their wickedness."* Paul begins his section on evil by rightly dividing the very nature of wickedness or sin. Essentially, he is making a distinction between slavery and rebellion. In the 'fall', and ever since the 'fall', mankind has been enslaved by sin. Jesus' well-known statement on sin and slavery in John 8:

Then you will know the truth, and the truth will set you free."
(John 8:32)

Free from what? Free from sinning! Sinning enslaves. It has since the Garden. But God, in his great mercy has provided a way of escape and reconciliation, *'while we were yet sinners'*. God, and his Son, took on the burden of man's sin in their own flesh. In one sense, sin is no longer a problem. Forgiveness and reconciliation have been provided for mankind, and done so at a great price.

But here in Romans Paul is making a distinction between sorrowful sinning and rebellion. God understands the fallen nature of man. It is part of mankind's childhood. For a season God has burdened man with **hard service**. It is punishment with a purpose. This sin burden will instill in man the need to draw close to God for his life and salvation.

However, and listen closely here; you can be forgiven and still be enslaved. Forgiveness does not free us from sin, the truth does. *'The truth will set you free'*. Truth is the underlying goal of the *Restoration* as we have noted along our journey. End-of-the-age prophecy is not so much about sin as it is about rebellion. And it is not so much about enslavement as it is about freedom.

Seeking Truth

In a sense, conforming to 'truth' is the second salvation. Discovering truth is man's (expected) response to God's gracious provision for sin. Man must transform his thinking, his perception of reality. Truth is defined as reality—that which is the case rather than that which is assumed. Can the kingdom of God be built upon a people who have a distorted understanding of reality? Empathically no!

In a free society like America (ideally), righteousness starts in the people; it is not imposed from above. America's original constitutional government was top-light and local.

Note this quote from John Adams, the second President of the United States, and the first Vice President, on October 11, 1798:

"Our Constitution was made only for a moral and religious people. It is wholly inadequate to the government of any other."

Why? Because a 'free constitution' (a minimal, non-authoritarian government) requires a self–governed population. The less self-governed (by truth) the population is, the greater the need for big, authoritarian government. People who won't righteously govern themselves seek kings to do so (1 Samuel 8). And big authoritarian government never works out well for the people. Just look how it worked out with King Saul.

The kingdom of God is no different. In the kingdom, the authority (RULERS) have largely a judicial function, defining righteousness, rather than enforcing righteousness.

This is why truth is the essential ingredient of the kingdom. Truth is the antidote for sinning (not forgiveness). When all is said and done Paul ends the prophetic portion of Romans with a truth statement...

And be not conformed to this world: but be ye transformed by the renewing of your mind, that ye may prove what [is] that good, and acceptable, and perfect, will of God. (Romans 12:2 KJV)

For those willing, transformed thinking is the objective. Jesus also stressed this truth objective in his last night as a flesh and blood human, in the Upper Room Discourse:

But when he, the Spirit of truth, comes, he will guide you into all the truth. (John 16:13 NIV)

The kingdom must be built on a people committed to truth. A people who accept truth, not power, as the foundation of government.

That hunger for truth must come from man's deepest faculties, from his mind, his heart, and his will. This is part of his spiritual makeup. Man is a truth being. If he does not possess truth, if he does not seek truth, he is not human. If he rejects truth, he is rejecting his humanity.

Truth Detection

Innate characteristics like conscience and truth come with the human package, being made in the image of God. Yes, but...

"all have sinned and fall short of the glory of God." (Romans 3:23)

The 'fall' and sin may dull these faculties, but have not negated them completely. The creation is truthful. So, even without understanding the law and sin, every man is accountable. Every man, even sinful man, is born with a built-in truth-detector—his sense of beauty and his conscience. One does not have to be a trained musician to detect a bad note, or an artist to see a flaw in a pattern.

Our sense of truth is given as part of the human essence. These truth faculties of man complement the Spirit of God in man's communion with God, and in the work of managing creation (or at least they will again someday).

Adam's first assignment was discerning truth in creation. It was his first task to discern the nature of each animal and give it a name that reflected such.

The Creation Gospel

Even in his fallen state, every man hears a 'creation gospel' to which he is accountable.

> For since the creation of the world God's invisible qualities--his eternal power and divine nature--have been clearly seen, being understood from what has been made, so that men are without excuse. (Romans 1:20)

Paul begins his argument with the creation gospel. If one is not true to the creation gospel, he will not be true to the kingdom gospel.

Restoring mankind is not only an issue of sin, even more so, it is an issue of truth. 'Truthlessness' will condemn you. Nature/creation is the first teacher of truth.

But a man can assault theses faculties of truth and conscience until they no longer serve him or mankind. They can become dead and useless as faculties of ministry or self-governance. By ultimately rejecting truth, a segment of mankind no longer serves their purpose as human (in the human body we call this cancer). Healthy 'cells' mutate and become destructive. They are REBELS and must be removed from the human race, assigned to everlasting fire, a fire that was never meant for humans:

> Then shall he say also unto them on the left hand, Depart from me, ye cursed, into everlasting fire, prepared for the devil and his angels: (Matthew 25:41 KJV)

The Cycle of Doom

In Romans 1 Paul makes a distinction between those caught in sin (aren't we all) and those who suppress the truth in their sinning. There is a difference. It becomes apparent that there is forgiveness for sinning; there is a cure for this disease. But there is ultimately no forgiveness for rejecting the truth, for not responding positively to the core attribute of being human.

Let me say that again, as this is essential to understand. There is forgiveness for sinning; but there is no forgiveness for rejecting the truth. Truthlessness is not redeemable; it is intentional, willful rebellion. Paul brilliantly begins to dissect this terrifying process of suppressing the truth, exchanging the truth for lies (1:25), and finally rejecting the truth (2:8), here in Romans.

He lists five steps to this 'cycle of doom', starting with futile thinking, infecting, and finally wholly corrupting, the human soul. Follow the narrative from Romans 1 below:

For although they knew God, they neither glorified him as God nor gave thanks to him, but their <u>thinking became futile</u> and their <u>foolish hearts were darkened</u>. Although they claimed to be wise, they became fools... (Verses 21, 22)

Therefore God gave them over in the <u>sinful desires</u> of their hearts to sexual impurity for the degrading of their bodies with one another. (Verse 24)

Because of this, God gave them over to <u>shameful lusts</u>. Even their women exchanged natural relations for unnatural ones. In the same way the men also abandoned natural relations with women and were inflamed with lust for one another. Men committed indecent acts with other men and received in themselves the due penalty for their perversion. Furthermore, since they did not think it worthwhile to retain the knowledge of God, he gave them over to a <u>depraved mind</u>, to do what ought not to be done. They have become filled with every kind of *wickedness, evil, greed and depravity. They are full of... (Verses 26-29)*

Here is a summary of the cycle of doom and the human faculty affecting it:

- futile thinking........ mind
- hearts darkened...... heart
- sinful desires......... heart
- shameful lusts........ heart
- depraved mind....... mind

Also, some other key phrases along the way:

"Although they claimed to be wise, they became fools" (1:21)

"Therefore God gave them over..." (1:24)

"They have become filled with every kind of wickedness..."(1:29)

Male, Female, and Sexuality

To illustrate his point, Paul wraps his argument around what is perhaps the most evident and striking reality in creation—male, female, and sexuality. There is nothing in creation more apparent than the complementary beauty and distinctions of male and female. 'Mommy' and 'daddy' are often the first words spoken by a baby. As one matures, those distinctions become even more pronounced.

This is not cultural, nor Biblical, it is intrinsic to creation and mankind. The reality of there being male and female is really 'Chapter One' in the creation gospel. Interestingly, it is also Chapter One in the written gospel as well.

So God created man in his [own] image, in the image of God created he him; male and female created he them. (Genesis 1:27 KJV)

'Man' is a composite of both male and female traits. The mind and the heart have gender characteristics. As we saw in the 'cycle of doom' above, Paul addresses both these internal gender distinctions in man's personality, as well as the external biological gender roles of mankind in his polemic.

It is interesting to note that science today has confirmed the Biblical account of 'Eve' being taken out of 'Adam'. Males have both female (X) and male (Y) sex chromosomes (XY), while females have only female (X) chromosomes (XX).

Humans are a fascinating mix of male and female. The male is a composite of both sex traits, the female traits being recessive. When both (X) and (Y) chromosomes are present the human is male. However, females require two female chromosomes and no male chromosomes, they are purely female. Male and female traits are complementary but not interchangeable. This is why a common idiom for males has developed as: "get in touch with your feminine side", but we see no such idiom for females to 'get in touch with their male side'.

It is becoming for a male to modestly integrate feminine traits into his own. Notice the 'fruit of the Spirit':

> *But the fruit of the Spirit is love, joy, peace, patience, kindness, goodness, faithfulness, gentleness and self-control. Against such things there is no law. (Galatians 5:22-23)*

This fruit is more naturally associated with female. It is quite apparent that a female is born with this fruit in greater measure. This gives us a very important insight into the prophetic nature of the male. Why does he have a female side; what is God's purpose in this?

It is not hard to see God's beautiful intent. A man's life work is to reintegrate the 'fruit' that was diminished when Eve was separated from him. But in an even greater way.

The female is the 'help-mate', the 'assistant builder', of a greater man. Woman, in a sense, is biologically perfect. She is born with an advanced compliment of spiritual resources. Much of her personality is intuitive. Man, on the other hand, needs to be built. He has feminine place-holders and various degrees of 'gifts' of the Spirit, but he needs 'construction' to be complete. His gifts are not biological, they are spiritual (divine), and they are acquired intentionally and forcefully. For him, it takes more time and the 'hard knocks' of life, to become 'a man'. In much of this, woman's biological perfections are his model in his journey to spiritual perfection in the Holy Spirit. Her female fruit is his example, helping him moderate and enhance his dominant male traits. Even the science of chromosomes can teach us a lesson in perfection.

But we don't need today's science to discover and understand the obvious roles of male and female—some things are self-evident. Today we have evidence from both biology and theology. Even the ideological foundation of the United States rests on self-evident truth.

So, whether spoken in the language of nature (the creation gospel) or the Bible (the written gospel), the issue is clear. Distinct gender roles are physical, spiritual, and critical. There is no more appropriate evidence of evil than the rejection of gender truth.

This is Paul's approach. He tells us, that after failing to properly glorify God, man begins an idolatrous process of replacing God with created things. Chief among them, perverted sex— 'exchanging natural relations for unnatural ones'.

Paul limits his arguments to the creation gospel, 'what is natural'. He doesn't quote Scripture to make his point. He could have, of course. There are authoritative Scriptures against what we today have come to call homosexual behavior. Paul seems to be saying, Scripture should not even be necessary. A naturally instinctive sense of truth should be enough.

We should sense that homosexuality is not wrong because God says it is wrong; it's wrong because it is untruthful. You don't need the Bible to know homosexuality is bad music. Without conditioning, virtually all men are extremely repulsed by any intimacy with another man.

The male/female model is a life giving and sustaining, holiness structure. A male/male model is not. In principle, homosexuality is parasitic; it cannot even support itself. A homosexual union is a biological dead-end. All homosexuals themselves are products of a heterosexual union. At best, homosexuality can only mimic the male/female model.

Essentially, there is no such thing as same-sex sex. It's like believing you can have a battery with two positive poles—impossible. No current would flow in such a battery, and the same is true of 'homo' (man-to-man) sexuality. There is no current in purely male to male sexuality. So, instead, both 'men' must pretend to be something they're not. One man acts the role of a woman, and the other is a man who prefers to have sex with a woman-mimicking man rather than a real woman. What a perversion of truth.

And yet, the truth war is in full bloom. America and the world is experiencing an anti-truth assault from every cultural venue. Truth is being turned on its head with some of the most irrational concepts imaginable. Image by image, truth and reality are being replaced with lies. We, and especially the young, are being desensitized to truth.

It doesn't happen overnight. The stages Paul describes above are happening right before our eyes: futile thinking, hearts darkened, sinful desires, shameful lusts, depraved minds.

It's not surprising that Paul uses homosexuality as the banner of moral decline. But of course, it's not the only sin. This is a package deal. Paul goes on to specifically list a full spectrum of wickedness.

They have become filled with every kind of wickedness... they are full of... (Romans 1:29)

This is the end of people who suppress the truth—full of... A kind of 'perfection of wickedness'. The terrifying part is that it is not solely voluntary. Three times Paul warns, '*God gives them over*', '*God gives them over', 'God gives them over'.* Futile thinking will eventually close the curtain on their humanity. The process is complete:

Corrupting the whole man—mind and heart.

Perverting the whole man—male and female.

But as we noted at the beginning of this section, Paul is making a distinction between sinning and rebellion, and homosexuality is the perfect device to make this distinction.

In a somewhat healthy culture, for example early America, the incidence of homosexuality is extremely low.   The cause of homosexuality is hotly debated. Homosexuality is certainly not part of God's original intent. And if someone rejects special creation, they will find no encouragement from evolution either. Even evolution (if it were accepted as true) has produced no life from male-to-male intimacy. Even evolution has found no way of producing anything more than a biological dead-end.

But in a fallen creation, various biological, environmental, and familial factors can contribute to this condition.

As adults, we are very much a product of our childhood environment (though not without choice). It only takes the smallest event, at a critical moment in childhood, or a prolonged deficiency, to program us with a predisposition for life. It is reasonable to acknowledge the existence of same-sex attractions independent of choice or full awareness.

Life may progress without proper guidance, or even with pernicious encouragement. Impure compulsions become lifestyle before a clear accounting is taken. In this world, it is not hard to find oneself driven by any number of 'unnatural' behaviors, sexual and otherwise.

But in quiet moments that inner voice grows louder. One has to make a choice: call evil good, or acknowledge sin for what it is; let one's heart grow darker, or seek forgiveness and deliverance. Ideally, one finds the grace and forgiveness of God.

But a struggle is not a loss. Homosexuality is the perverting of a natural inclination toward a loving relationship. Even while enslaved and overcome by these attractions, there is God's mercy. The temptation is to redefine the standard, the 'law', to replace it with society's values. No, never, never, reject or diminish that inner 'law'.

> *The law was added so that the trespass might increase. But where sin increased, grace increased all the more... (Romans 5: 20)*

Rather, call upon God's mercy and grace. Sorrowful sinning is a state we all find ourselves in. Whether it be sinful sexual behavior, overeating, gossip, lying, or any of the myriad other acts of disobedience. Our goal should be to walk perfectly, but there is forgiveness and mercy when we fall short. This is true for homosexuality as well.

Someone caught in the snare of homosexuality is not the direct focus of Paul's dissertation on evil. It is not regretful 'doers' that Paul chastises here, it is the 'approvers' that are the real face of evil. It is those that: "*suppress the truth by their wickedness.*"

Homosexuality invades a culture not by homosexuals, who are relatively few, but by the 'approvers'—those having no homosexual proclivity, yet purposely affirm such behavior, and thereby advancing the war against truth. This is the distinction Paul is making here.

The REBELS are not those caught in the grip of human weaknesses. The mercy and grace of God can forgive and restore penitent sinners. The REBELS are those who have rejected the clear gospel of creation; thereby, rejecting what it means to be human. Intentionally equating the beautiful, life giving, and sustaining role of male and female, with a same-sex relationship, is clear evidence of rejecting the truth. This is Paul's bottom line.

When has so much been said in just fifteen verses? It is Paul's first lesson in perfection—the perfection of evil. In the next seven chapters, he will trace the development of those who will achieve another perfection, a harvest of righteousness; these are the RULERS who will be conformed to the likeness of God's Son (Romans 8:29).

These are two of the 'perfections' achieved by humanity in the first generation of the Millennium. Achieving this final 'harvest' of human character, at both ends of the spectrum, is the purpose of the *Restoration*.

RULERS

Chapters 2 thru 8, which is the heart of Romans, focuses on the sons of God, the RULERS. Then Paul will shift to 'my people' in chapters 9-11, the CITIZENS.

It is interesting to note the personal pronouns Paul uses to relate with each group respectively; Chapter 1: they/them; Chapters 2-8: we/you/us; Chapters 9-11: they/them. Paul identifies with the middle group, the sons of God, even while his heart cries out for 'my people', the CITIZENS.

It's important to notice a distinction between these two groups. The CITIZENS, after a season of 'stumbling' (9:32), '*all Israel will be saved*' (11:26). Note that this 'salvation' is AFTER and NOT part of the revealing of the sons (the RULERS) in chapter 8. This is CITIZEN salvation—an eternal, earthly kingdom (of David)—just what Israel (Judaism) has been promised, and is looking for.

The REBELS are represented by the unrepentant thief in the scene on Calvary. Most Christians would identify with the thief that repented at the last minute. But, as a prophetic type, the repentant thief is a CITIZEN (although he may personally, by grace, become a RULER). This repentant thief is NOT a picture of the final work of Jesus and the Holy Spirit in his people. This thief depicts a belated surrender to God's mercies and his salvation. As a prophetic type, he is neither an overcomer, nor a partner in Jesus' ministry.

So, the two thieves represent the REBELS and the CITIZENS. Which cross represents the RULERS? Earlier we talked about how the Melchizedek priesthood was necessary to provide victory and the perfection of the saints. It is not simply about getting into heaven by grace, but, by grace, attaining to the fullness, stature, and image of Christ—in other words perfection. Some men, following in the likeness of their Lord, will master sin here on earth while yet 'flesh and blood', AND perform a perfect 'greater works' ministry.

RULER salvation offers the 'new creation'—a mysterious 'new nature' that comes with being born-again. In the new creation, we have been given the potential for real freedom, an escape from sinning. But, this final journey to all-truth and freedom (from sinning) must come from our response to this grace. Ultimately, the RULERS will hear the words of the master, *"Well done, good and faithful servant*; (Matthew 25:23).

The sons of God are not represented by the repentant thief on the cross. Looking a little closer, we see there are effectively two men on that middle cross—Jesus and I (if I intend to rule and reign with him). *"We died with Christ'* (Romans 6:8). Our final perfection, provided by the work of Christ, will be as complete as Christ's (Ephesians 4:11-13). Also, notice that two men carried that cross to Calvary (Matthew 27:32), and two men 'died' on that middle cross.

A short side note: There is an extremely faulty definition of grace in parts of Christianity. (Hyper) grace is wrongly defined as an unlimited provision for man's failure; unlimited forgiveness. One has to wonder where an idea like this comes from, certainly not the Bible. Even human parents would not tolerate this in their children much less our righteous heavenly Father. His children, those made in his image, will be victorious. True grace <u>accommodates failure only in the process of creating perfection</u>. True grace is 'the power to change'; 'the power to reach perfection'. That is the story of Romans.

Romans 8, the pinnacle of the book, describes the final state of the sons. Their end is not depicted as pardoned 'thieves'. They are depicted as overcomers. We were *"predestined to be conformed to the image of his Son"* (8:29). This is not justification found way back in Chapters 3 & 4. No, in Chapter 8, we have CONFORMITY, a harvest of righteousness—honest-to-goodness sinless perfection.

CITIZENS

As Paul finishes the story of the REBELS and RULERS, he finally turns to describe the third people group (CITIZENS) in chapters 9-11, his 'my people' (by blood, not identity). Here, as he reaches the third people group, he can paint for us the big picture of God's sovereign plan for mankind:

> *Does not the potter have the right to make out of the same lump of clay some pottery for* <u>special purposes</u> *and some for* <u>common use</u>*? What if God, although choosing to show his wrath and make his power known, bore with great patience the* <u>objects of his wrath</u>*--prepared for destruction? (Romans 9:21-22)*

In these verses Paul clearly summarizes his thinking on three people groups–RULERS, CITIZENS, and REBELS. In the Epistle to the Philippians he reveals a similar picture stated in different terms:

> *That at the name of Jesus every knee should bow, of [things] in* <u>heaven</u>*, and [things] in* <u>earth</u>*, and [things]* <u>under the earth</u>*; (Phil. 2:10)*

Here again Paul identifies the three universal jurisdictions of moral creatures. The three destinies of human beings—heaven, earth, and hell.

It is vital to build a prophetic model around three people groups (RULERS, CITIZENS and REBELS), rather than two (RULERS and REBELS). If we don't get our people groups right, we will certainly get our prophecy wrong.

In Romans we see the magnificent journey of mankind as revealed in their full flowering, all three people groups. Yes, some stumbled and fell, and some will remain REBELS to the very end. But that is the minor story of mankind. The major story is that some have faith and some have faith plus blood. There are two eternally living groups of mankind. Some have 'everlasting life' and some have 'immortal life'. They will both prove to be victorious in their own ways.

Chapter Twelve

THREE PEOPLE GROUPS IN THE OLIVET DISCOURSE

And, finally, we return to Jesus' own words concerning three people groups in the Olivet Discourse. Each commission in Matthew 24 (v.14 and v.45) is directed at the identity of, and/or the ministry of, people groups.

Beside the two commissions in chapter 24, the Olivet Discourse has three parables in chapter 25. The structure of the Olivet Discourse is curious. Chapter 24 is all prophetic narrative while Chapter 25 consists of three distinct parables. They are closely related. It is likely that in Jesus' original presentation he inserted the three Matthew 25 parables within the context of his message in Matthew 24, but when they were recorded for us by the writers, the parables were added as a group on the end. The three parables are:

1. The Wise and Foolish Virgins
2. The Talents
3. The Sheep and the Goats

Prophetically, they are in chronological order. The key narrative portions in Matthew 24—the Exodus, the wilderness journey, and the Promised Land entry, directly relate to the three parables in Matthew 25, respectively.

It is quite shocking to see how Christian commentaries are unable, and apparently even unconcerned, about finding a systematic framework for interpreting this critical, prophetic sermon, considering the monolithic sermon that it is. The intent of the sermon was a systematic prophetic overview, NOT a mostly unrelated collection of aids for 'Today's Christian Living'.

A Quick Review

The Discourse opens with the first commission (verse 14), an Exodus event, which begins the *Restoration*. The Exodus event includes the revealing or setting-apart of the sons of God (RULERS) for their perfecting and final ministry, which comes much later. At this time, the world as we know it, is also 'ended' and 'reset' as described earlier in this book.

This triggers a 'first generation', of humans who will choose one of three identities. They will be born into a new 'Sabbath' spiritual environment (an environment free of original sin).

The very purpose of the *Restoration* generation is to identify, separate, and harvest the full potential of each human group (for good or evil); and to facilitate the 'adult' (final) expression of each group.

> *I tell you the truth, this generation (of three people groups) will certainly not pass away until all these things (Restoration) have happened. (Matthew 24:34)*

In the last fourteen years of the *Restoration*, the RULER group, those 'faithful and wise' sons, will manage a worldwide '*Joseph* commission' (v. 45). This final season will be patterned after the Joseph story. Seven years of great prosperity, followed by near fatal famine, is designed to 'reveal' the CITIZEN and REBEL groups and bring them to 'maturity' (bring CITIZENS under the covenant, etc.).

So, we see the vital role of these two commissions, and why Jesus highlighted them in his end-of-the-age *Restoration* survey. Adding to our understanding of these events, we have many parables. Virtually all parables have the intent of dividing people groups, thus distinguishing one group from another. Notable among them is the Parable of the Wheat and the Tares in Matthew 13, which is a parable directly addressing the Matthew 24:14 'end' (Exodus) event.

We now recognize that the key elements of Matthew 24 are designed around identifying and maturing the three people groups. The three parables in chapter 25 will add to our understanding of this process.

Remember, in this book we have not given extensive background arguments to many of the core issues. Rather, our purpose here is to state the issues as clearly and succinctly as possible. Future works will add much greater detail.

The Wise and Foolish Virgins Parable

Moving on to the parables in Matthew 25, the chapter begins with the Parable of the Wise and Foolish Virgins. This first parable corresponds to the first commission in Matthew 24:14, the Exodus event.

We notice first that they are all 'virgins'. This implies that both groups are 'good' people groups in our terms. The essence of the parable is: some have prepared adequately (for the wedding) and some have not.

This virgins/wedding parable gives prophetic clarity (as we did earlier) to the Exodus; there are really two groups that leave for the Promised Land. Prophetically speaking, some are 'saved' by the blood (firstborns, a spiritual wise choice) and some are just 'saved' from Egypt and bondage.

Three months later, the gathering at Mt. Sinai is a type of wedding (or engagement) ceremony where the Mosaic covenant, is offered. It is effectively a ketubah, a special Jewish prenuptial agreement in preparation for marriage. This ketubah is offered to the people who say

'I do', and is affirmed by sprinkling them with the *'blood of the covenant'* (Ex. 24:8).

Prophetically, those who are truly prepared to participate in the wedding say 'I do'; these are the wise virgins. Also, notice the punishment of the foolish virgins. It does not say they are 'cast into outer darkness' like the punishment in the Talents parable (25:30). They are simply not allowed to participate in the wedding (they effectively don't become the bride).

Notice the phrase, 'and the door was shut'. This implies, as we noted earlier, the end of 'go to heaven' (wedding) salvation. RULER salvation is closed at the 'revealing of the sons of God' (Exodus). There may be exceptions, but generally it can be assumed the 'salvation' being proclaimed for the last 2000 years as 'the gospel' is over. The 'sons of God' are identified, leave the world, and retreat (or advance) into the wilderness for a time of isolated preparation/restoration. They are 'corporately complete', except for the children of the 'first generation' born to them.

Here, the theological corporate structures known as 'the Bride', 'the Spiritual Temple', 'the Melchizedek Priesthood', etc. (these are the same corporate body with different functions) are perfected and prepared for service.

'Salvation' after this point is NOT 'into Christ' but into eternal human life (on earth). The foolish virgins in this parable are denied RULER salvation, but may experience eternal human life (by eating from the tree of life, Revelation 22) if they are CITIZENS of the kingdom. They are 'foolish' only in the relative sense of not *'gaining the incomparable riches of Christ'* (Ephesians 2:4-7, 1 Peter 5:10).

The Parable of the Talents

There are several things to keep in mind when addressing this next parable. First, it is part of a monolithic sermon, not an isolated insight.

Second, it is part of a PROPHETIC sermon, not a PASTORAL sermon, which unfortunately is the emphasis of all Christian commentaries.

And since the parable revolves around 'talents', it would make sense to ask: what are the talents? Since we are expecting prophetic revelation here, one can assume the talents are NOT 'money' or 'talents' (special natural abilities or aptitudes), which are pastoral concerns.

That may leave a difficult search for a proper interpretation. But a very plausible explanation comes from the 'punch line' of the parable itself:

> *For everyone who has will be given more, and he will have an abundance. Whoever does not have, even what he has will be taken from him. (Matthew 25:29)*

Earlier, in the parables of Matthew 13, Jesus himself uses and interprets this phrase for us:

> *He replied, "Because the knowledge of the <u>secrets of the kingdom of heaven</u> has been given to you, but not to them. Whoever has will be given more, and they will have an abundance. Whoever does not have, even what they have will be taken from them. (Matthew 13:11-12)*

So, it is quite evident that the talents are the 'secrets of the kingdom'. The 'secrets' are a prophetic asset. But applying this to the specific prophetic context or event in the Olivet Discourse may still prove to be difficult.

We already discovered that the framework for the whole Olivet Discourse is the prophetic journey from Egypt into the Promised Land. The first commission relates to the beginning event, the Exodus. The second commission relates to the last events of the *Restoration*. Therefore, if the parables are in chronological order, it is reasonable to assume that this Talents parable may be related to the wilderness period of the journey.

In principle, the Talents parable is about an issue we covered earlier, and a major theme of this whole Millennium commissions presentation – human initiative. Specifically, it is about the sons of God discovering a full and complete understanding of the kingdom. By investing in given kingdom secrets, the sons of God will piece together all the secrets of the kingdom.

Resolving 'all-truth' is one of the objectives Jesus assigns to us in the Upper Room Discourse.

> *"I have much more to say to you, more than you can now bear. But when he, the Spirit of truth, comes, he will guide you into ALL-TRUTH. He will not speak on his own; he will speak only what he hears, and he will tell you what is yet to come." (John 16:12-13)*

Jesus had much more he 'could' have said to us. But that wasn't in God's design. Jesus said enough, and enough has been written down for us, that we can resolve 'all-truth'. But it is the Holy Spirit, the still quiet voice of the Spirit, which will lead us into all-truth (during the 2000-year wilderness journey, by the way). Through individual and corporate prayer and study we will take what we have been given and piece together the complex 'puzzle' of reality. As we said earlier, 'the Bible is all true, but it is not all-truth'. All-truth comes via Spirit-led human initiative.

That is the principle Jesus is stressing in the Talents parable. God has given us (not all mankind, only the sons of God) some 'truths' (two and five talents here), and he is expecting us to resolve 'all-truth'. This is not only the son's heritage, it is their responsibility.

This is not a casual issue! Take note of the advice and attitude of many 'experts'. They say: "Do not go beyond Scripture; the Bible warns against 'adding' to Scripture. Scripture, and Scripture alone, is our safe place. Do not go beyond the written Word."

Well, at best this is poor advice against error. The science of truth-detecting is a fascinating one which we will not go into here. But, how do we gain (all) truth? Well, one way that positively won't work is to 'lock up the truth' we already have, having the attitude that an unblemished half-truth is far safer than reaching for (a potentially) dangerous or imperfect all-truth.

We must realize that half-truth can be all true, and yet a lie (hyper-grace for instance). We may find ourselves guilty of defending falsity. The real answer to deception or error is the vigorous pursuit of all-truth—and that is our goal.

Using caution can be well intentioned (the servant given one talent), but this parable warns us of the potential down-side. Under the guise of 'defending the truth' is the potential for an evil 'minimalist' attitude toward the full spectrum of God's purposes. An evil heart may choose to go just far enough. 'Our truth' is enough, most of Christianity says, ignoring Jesus commands/promises such as 'one body' and 'all-truth'. The ONLY assurance that 'our truth' is enough, is all-truth (and we could add, prophetic truth). The ONLY assurance our 'five talents' are correct is discovering five more, as Jesus commanded.

One can choose to 'go to heaven' (get fire insurance) and not be concerned about God's will being done on earth.

All told, we have been given the assignment to conquer and settle the 'Promised Land'. The sons of God have no material inheritance in this earth, as such. Their 'Promised Land' is a relationship grounded in CONFORMITY to their master Jesus, to become, really become, like him, to go all the way; to enter a Sabbath-rest.

This responsibility is not just for our good, but for the benefit of the people of earth (CITIZENS). The beginning of the Book of Hebrews also deals with this attitude—a wicked wilderness attitude. It's not a coincidence that the setting for this Hebrew's warning is 'the journey'.

So, as the Holy Spirit says: "Today, if you hear his voice, do not harden your hearts as you did in the rebellion, during the time of testing in the wilderness, where your ancestors tested and tried

> *me, though for forty years they saw what I did. That is why I was angry with that generation; I said, 'Their hearts are always going astray, and they have not known my ways.' So I declared on oath in my anger, 'They shall never enter my rest.' " ... So we see that they were not able to enter, because of their unbelief. [Hebrews 3:7-11, 19]*

The Parable of the Talents deals with this issue. Today, our journey is not material, it is spiritual. It is not to heaven, it is the conquest of all-truth—which must be expressed within the context of the kingdom manifested on earth (for the CITIZENS).

Do we care about truth? Honestly, have you ever heard a sermon on all-truth? How will we build an enduring kingdom on earth while lacking truth? Our attitude about the 'talents' will speak to that issue. Are we faithful servants? Are we investing the 'secrets' we have been given toward the hope we have been promised? Are we prepared to bring a Millennium-rest (Sabbath-rest) to this earth? No one else will do it.

The three parables of Matthew 25 are directed at the people groups. The first parable, the 'Wise and Foolish Virgins', begins to define who the RULERS are within the context of an Exodus. That refinement continues with the parable of the Talents and the expectation of acquiring all-truth. The last parable speaks to the final resolution of our *Joseph* ministry (before resurrection) identifying CITIZENS and REBELS (sheep and goats). Each of the three parables gives us progressive insights on the journey to the Promised Land and the final kingdom.

Two Talents?

In a very real sense this book testifies to the fulfilment of the parable of the talents. As we have repeated innumerable times, the prophecy model revealed in this book rests on two commissions discovered in Mathew 24—the 'Exodus' commission (v.14), and the 'Joseph' commission (v.45). These two foundational 'talents', or 'secrets of the kingdom', were specifically given by the 'master', just days before he left on a 'long journey'. In the interim, the master's servants have been busy creating a vast body of eschatological knowledge built up over 2000 years of study.

Now recently the Spirit of prophecy has been blowing stronger in the servants' hearts. We have now come to fully understand these two 'talents' given to us by the 'master'. With them, we have multiplied kingdom secrets and can now create a complete prophetic model of the end-of-the-age just as the 'master' has told us.

'For to everyone who has, more will be given, and he will have abundance' (v25:29)

It is our sincere hope that when he returns, we will be able to say to him,

'Master, you entrusted us with five talents. See, we have gained five more.' (v25:20)

And then, of course, to hear those blessed words, '*Well done, good and faithful servant!*' (v25:21,23)

Chapter Thirteen

THE SHEEP AND THE GOATS PARABLE

And finally, in our search to discover three people groups, we have come to the Sheep and the Goats Parable. This is not technically a parable (although we'll continue to refer to it as a parable). It is simply the description of a literal future event, and it should be treated as literal prophecy, rather than the more abstract and subjective mode of a parable. The people involved are simply referred to as being 'separated as sheep and goats', distinguished primarily by their final identity, and how they came to be part of that group. Here is the beginning of the account:

> "When the Son of Man comes in his glory, and all the angels with him, he will sit on his glorious throne. All the nations will be gathered before him, and he will separate the people one from another as a shepherd separates the sheep from the goats. (Matthew 25:31-32)

"*When the Son of Man comes in his glory...*" This phrase clearly gives us the timing for this parable—shortly after the literal, physical, coming of Messiah Jesus to earth. The Sheep and the Goats Parable is a post resurrection, post second-coming event.

At Messiah's coming, after all the dust settles, the likely first item of business will be a final cleanup. This cleanup will involve a trial-like adjudication that will determine the immediate and eternal destiny of two groups of people. It will be a judgment of the living only, the people of the nations; what is left of the first generation of the Millennium. All human beings alive at that time will be "evaluated" and a simple live or die ruling will be decreed for each person.

Those adjudicated for life (sheep) will be the human people group (in our terminology, CITIZENS) who (along with their future children) will populate the earth during the thousand-year Millennium. The 'goats' are the REBEL people group (in our terms), somehow eliminated from among the living.

A casual view of this parable would seem to support a simple two people group model. In traditional Christian terminology, and virtually all Christian commentary on this parable, these sheep are 'saved', and today's Christianity only knows one type of salvation. That means they are declared to be part of the 'go to heaven', 'in Christ', 'glorified body' people group (RULERS, in our terms). So, Christian thinking here is that this Sheep and Goats Parable is straightforward judgment of the living—who is 'saved' and who is 'lost'.

Perhaps that is your judgment as well. If you haven't really thought about it, or formed a studied opinion, please stop, and take the time to do so now. It's complicated, but it's important. As we will see, this parable presents a clear challenge, like few others, to both traditional theological and prophetic Christian views. It should quicken an appetite for healthier prophetic fare.

A Radical Challenge to Christian Tradition

On the surface, in this parable, we are seeing traditional Christian pre-resurrection salvation imagery. It is consistent with a two-thousand-year Great Commission tradition, proclaiming the need of all men for 'salvation', a salvation by grace through faith, provided by the life and substitutionary death of Jesus the Messiah.

But this parable takes on a whole different meaning when a larger and more accurate context is taken into account.

Of the three dozen or so parables in the NT, this parable is unique in its prophetic message to us. It is the only parable with a post resurrection and a post second-coming context. And, even more important, it is the only parable with a primary focus on the CITIZENS group.

It is directed toward the Millennium CITIZENS who are the primary, in fact the only, flesh and blood citizens of earth. Interestingly, the Book of Romans follows this same pattern. After the sons of God are revealed (Ch. 8), the focus changes and Paul turns his attention to the CITIZENS (Ch. 9-11). Both Paul, in the book of Romans, and Jesus, end their prophetic survey with the CITIZENS.

Our objective in this section of our essay is to identify the three people groups. Two are well known, of course, but this last parable of Jesus uniquely confronts Christianity's faulty 'two people group' theology. Discovering a third people group is essential to understanding prophecy, and in particular, the purpose of the complex *Restoration* soon to come.

Most people have just not taken the time to look this far ahead in any detail. Think about the issue here in this parable; the mass-resurrection of the Saints (RULERS), both dead and living, has just happened. Every 'Saint' in the universe now has a glorified, immortal, super-human body and have become active full partners with Christ in his ongoing work. And yet we have this picture of the living sheep who are 'so-called' saved Saints (according to commentary). How can this work?

The Saints (all living and dead) have been newly resurrected, so one might casually think these saved 'sheep' (where did they come from?) will be resurrected later, perhaps at the end of the Millennium. But there is no evidence of any further individual or mass 'Saints'

(RULERS) resurrection. Our contention here is that at the resurrection of the RULERS, this group is eternally 'corporately complete'; membership is closed. All the corporate entities that designate RULERS, such as Body, Bride, Priesthood, Temple, Sons, etc. are finished and functional, never again to be added to numerically.

The RULERS are done. What the Parable points to is a new pathway for human civilization. Conceptually, it's not new. We have been making a theological case for it with our list of 'twos' (two sons, two covenants, two priesthoods, etc.). But now we have arrived, in this Parable of Jesus, at the flowering of a subtle truth of theological history.

To our list of twos we must now add two (and only two) distinct mass resurrections, with two body types, and two eternal salvations. From the beginning, this has been planned. Heaven and earth; two jurisdictions, with two governments, which are effectively manifested in two distinct yet harmonious kingdoms.

All this is finally laid bare by the sheep. After taking a closer look, we see in these sheep a third people group (CITIZENS), and a new, unknown type of 'salvation', a CITIZENS' salvation. Together these point to a government or kingdom on earth, separate from the RULERS. For the RULERS, they will begin their formal function as rulers, essentially performing judicial oversight ministered from within the divine family.

A short study on the general issue of resurrection will help us affirm these points and give us the knowledge we need to understand the issues behind the Sheep and the Goats Parable.

A Closer Look at Resurrection

As we said earlier, the Sheep and the Goats Parable is a post second-coming event. Therefore, the larger context of the parable, regularly overlooked, is the resurrection. It has just taken place days (or in some eschatology, a few years) earlier. (The time since the resurrection makes no difference for our argument here; we'll assume days).

The RULER resurrection has taken place, and the just-glorified Saints are now with Christ, as the special event is described in this Scripture:

> *For the Lord himself shall descend from heaven with a shout, with the voice of the archangel, and with the trump of God: and the dead in Christ shall rise first: Then we which are alive [and] remain shall be caught up together with them in the clouds, to meet the Lord in the air: and so shall we ever be with the Lord. (1 Thessalonians 4:16-17)*

This event is also commonly referred to as the Rapture. Attempting to avoid deep and muddy eschatological waters, we will just note the common debate of 'Christ coming FOR his saints' and 'Christ coming WITH his saints' as two separate events. For our purposes here, that distinction makes little difference; we will assume (as is likely the case) that they are essentially the same event, which we'll refer to here as the resurrection.

In both secular and Biblical terminology, resurrection is simply 'a raising up, or the act of rising from the dead'. The word in the New Testament is 'anastasis' (there is no such word in the OT). This very broad generic word has proven to be adequate for general theological discussions, but its very general use inhibits the resolution needed to understand greater prophetic issues adequately.

There are at least two different types of 'raisings' portrayed in the Bible that we, and the Bible, may generally refer to as resurrection. However, by studying this event more closely we will come to not only understand resurrection better, but we will gain a better insight into related issues. These have huge prophetic significance, particularly for our concern here—three people groups.

Two Types of Resurrections

As we said, the English word resurrection is translated from the Greek word 'anastasis'. But from the examples we have, that word seems to be applied to at least two different types of 'raising' from the dead, resulting in two distinct forms of physical bodies. It is only by carefully observing the context that we can distinguish these two events.

RULER Resurrection

One type of raising is clearly shown by the example of Jesus in which he is restored to life with a glorified, human-like, but supernatural body. This 'glorified' body, apparently looks like a typical human body, and has 'flesh'. But Paul teaches that:

'Not all flesh is the same' (I Corinthians 15:39).

There are also heavenly bodies and there are earthly bodies; but the splendor of the heavenly bodies is one kind, and the splendor of the earthly bodies is another. ... As was the earthly man, so are those who are of the earth; and as is the heavenly man, so also are those who are of heaven. (I Corinthians 15:40, 48)

So, we have resurrection into a glorified body. Here are several more Scriptures mentioning RULER resurrection.

But our citizenship is in heaven. And we eagerly await a Savior from there, the Lord Jesus Christ, who, by the power that enables him to bring everything under his control, will transform our lowly bodies so that they will be like his glorious body. (Philippians 3:20-21)

For in this we groan, earnestly desiring to be clothed upon with our house which is from heaven: (II Corinthians 5:2)

But, as of today, 2019, we only have one example of such a resurrection in human history.

CITIZEN Resurrection

A second type of raising from the dead, is demonstrated by the Biblical example of Lazarus, and others, who are restored to life in a natural, flesh and blood body, apparently identical to their former mortal body, and without some type of intervention, would die again. Here's Lazarus...

> When he had said this, Jesus called in a loud voice, "Lazarus, come out!" The dead man came out, his hands and feet wrapped with strips of linen, and a cloth around his face. Jesus said to them, "Take off the grave clothes and let him go." (John 11:43-44)

And another, where many are raised to life...

> And when Jesus had cried out again in a loud voice, he gave up his spirit. At that moment the curtain of the temple was torn in two from top to bottom. The earth shook and the rocks split. The tombs broke open and the bodies of many holy people who had died were raised to life. They came out of the tombs, and after Jesus' resurrection [raising, not anastasis] they went into the holy city and appeared to many people. (Matthew 27:50-53)

We have a limited number of examples of this type of resurrection in both Old and New Testaments. As far as we know, Lazarus and the other resurrected humans all died again sometime later.

We will examine each body type in greater detail below, but first...

Resurrection vs. Resuscitation

So, we need to differentiate both types of 'raisings'. If we apply the word 'resurrection' to a 'glorified', Jesus type resurrection, then we need to appropriate another word for this miracle of 'raising' back into a mortal body. For this discussion, perhaps a good word for this type of 'raising' would be 'resuscitation'.

With little forethought, the Christian world relates resurrection (into a glorified body) as the default 'raising'. This is clearly a Christian bias. The Greek word anastasis would most naturally apply to a resuscitation as defined above. Even the Greeks could imagine humans coming back to life after death. But a 'glorified life' has no precedent; no human (or angel) had ever seen such a thing.

Immortal, glorified resurrection is something neither the Greeks, nor even the Hebrews had a word for. It had never happened and, in reality, was probably never truly imagined. It starts to get a little complicated when the Bible uses the word resurrection for what appears to be both types of events.

The Hebrew Bible has very little to say about life after death. Judaism is very much about life here-and-now, on earth. In fact, one of the three major Jewish sects of Jesus' day, the Sadducees, did not believe in resurrection at all, or the immortality of the soul. We see the writer of Acts making note of this:

> *But when Paul perceived that the one part were Sadducees, and the other Pharisees, he cried out in the council, Men [and] brethren, I am a Pharisee, the son of a Pharisee: of the hope and resurrection of the dead I am called in question. ... For the Sadducees say that there is no resurrection, neither angel, nor spirit: but the Pharisees confess both. (Act 23:6, 8 KJV)*

After the destruction of the Temple in 70 AD the elite Sadducees largely disappeared. Today's Judaism is largely a spiritual descendant of the Pharisees, including belief in the resurrection, or, as we are defining it here, resuscitation. Judaism believed in a general resurrection in the world to come, though the specifics are somewhat poorly defined. Let's take a quick look at Judaism's prayer for resurrection in a Jewish prayer called the Amidah.

Jewish Resurrection – Amidah (Shmoneh Esreh)

The Amidah is the core of every Jewish siddur (prayer) service, and is therefore often referred to as HaTefillah, or "The prayer." Amidah, which literally means, "standing," refers to a series of blessings recited while standing. It was likely first developed by Ezra and the 'Great Assembly', a group of scholars and prophets, the forerunner of the Sanhedrin (hundreds of years before Jesus). This prayer (in its form then) would have been familiar to Jesus and the Apostles.

The Amidah is the most solemn prayer in the Jewish liturgy, also known as the 'shmonah esreh' ('eighteen blessings', today nineteen). It is repeated at each of three prayer services in a typical weekday: morning, afternoon, and evening, while standing. The prayer is composed of eighteen short prayers and praises directed at the resurrection, the restoration of Jerusalem, and the coming of the Messiah. Nothing should disturb the pious worshiper while he is engaged in this prayer.

The second blessing of the Amidah is called Gevurot ("mighty deeds"), and offers praise to God as the ultimate Power in the universe as demonstrated by the resurrection from the dead. Here is the second blessing:

> *You are mighty forever, my Lord; You resurrect the dead; You are powerful to save. He sustains the living with loving kindness, resurrects the dead with great mercy, supports the falling, heals the sick, releases the bound, and fulfills His trust to those who sleep in the dust. Who is like You, mighty One! And who can be compared to You, King, who brings death and restores life, and causes deliverance to spring forth! And you are faithful to*

resurrect the dead. Blessed are You, Lord who resurrects the dead.

Heaven on Earth

Jewish resurrection does not anticipate 'living in heaven' or the transformation to a glorified body. Their hope is essentially resuscitation and a glorious life on earth. The Old Testament has examples of individual resuscitations, but here is an Old Testament reference to a mass resurrection (resuscitation):

Multitudes who sleep in the dust of the earth will awake: some to everlasting life, others to shame and everlasting contempt. (Daniel 12:2)

This event is probably what Jesus was referring to when he said:

Marvel not at this: for the hour is coming, in which all that are in the graves shall hear his voice, and shall come forth; they that have done good, unto the resurrection of life; and they that have done evil, unto the resurrection of damnation. (John 5:28, 29)

We notice that the New Testament uses the word resurrection for this event, but on closer examination the context would most likely indicate resuscitation. The Bible often uses the 'sleep' metaphor for death, and 'awake' or 'arise' for returning to life. It is such a rare activity that precise words have not been developed.

But we need to think about the issue more precisely because it is not just about etymology. This distinction between resurrection and resuscitation is not nearly as relevant to vocabulary as it is to prophecy. We have already noted how Judaism is 'this-world' oriented. They have no concept of living in heaven; they see no need for that at all. Their promises from God were about land, peace, prosperity, and honor on this earth (although there are hints of something more profound).

If we had a peaceful, prosperous Garden of Eden here on earth, what more could man want? Man is made from the dust of this earth, he is uniquely designed and in harmony with paradise on earth—if he could ever attain it. In one sense, there is nothing better.

So, we see that the people group virtually invisible to Christian theology, the CITIZENS, is actually the default people group of the Bible, and of earth. For Christians, this may strike us as rather odd. Eternity on earth is the default promise? So where did Christians get all this talk of 'going to heaven'?

Kingdom of Heaven

At the beginning of the fourth prophetic 'day', along comes Jesus who preaches about the 'kingdom of heaven' (or kingdom of God). What is that? John, Jesus, and eventually the Apostles and the church would ultimately come preaching the gospel-of-the-kingdom of heaven. This kingdom was something beyond the Royal House of David, popularly anticipated by Israel. As this new sect of Judaism developed, which later came to be known as Christianity, it slowly took on a decidedly un-Jewish, other-worldly, perspective. Over the years, these two different perspectives clashed and eventually split.

Once again, we are beginning to distinguish two 'good' elements of God's creation—two people groups with two spiritual governments, eventually to become two living kingdoms. They clash only because they are immature. Ultimately, they will reach full maturity and work in harmony with each other. They relate to our first binary concepts of heaven and earth in Genesis.

A Closer Look at Two Body Types

Each resurrection type is an eternal identity with a distinct body type. Today, most Christians and Christian theology perceive resurrection in the mode of Christian resurrection, i.e. glorified immortal bodies. There appears to be no Old Testament model for the Christian 'glorified' resurrection. The Old Testament and today's Judaism are looking for a general resurrection, closer to what we are calling resuscitation. Both groups anticipate 'eternal-life', or living forever, but with significant differences.

To get a better idea of their distinctive characteristics and how they differ, yet harmonize in God's eternal plan, let's look a little closer at each.

As we've noted, the main distinguishing factor is that resurrection results in a supernatural immortal body, as opposed to resuscitation which produces a mortal body (that may or may not live forever). Someone resuscitated may die again, as in Lazarus' case, or experience the 'second death' as in those of the general resuscitation. (The 'second death' may have some aspects of immortality). Ideally, resurrection produces immortal life, and resuscitation produces eternal life.

Both are meant to be eternal, but the nature of that life is profoundly different. The RULERS, like Jesus, possess the intrinsic substance of divinity. They are immortal. How can one explain this indescribable privilege? One can't really; it is by the grace and goodness of God.

But it is only through these (millions of) RULERS that God, himself, will be truly manifested and known in the universe. That is why a whole generation of RULERS must be SELECTED and PERFECTED as an archetype generation, BEFORE resurrection and immortality. The question of disobedience or rebellion must be absolutely settled. Imagine the dilemma of immortalizing disobedience!

So, the RULERS actually exist as the substance of God; life apart from creation. The CITIZENS, on the other hand, remain human and mortal, but expect to live forever. How does this work?

Blood

Natural, mortal life, for men and animals is related to blood. God tells us that human (and animal) life is in the blood, note:

For the life of the flesh [is] in the blood: and I have given it to you upon the altar to make an atonement for your souls: for it [is] the blood [that] maketh an atonement for the soul. ... For [it is] the life of all flesh; the blood of it [is] for the life thereof: therefore I said unto the children of Israel, Ye shall eat the blood of no manner of flesh: for the life of all flesh [is] the blood thereof: whosoever eateth it shall be cut off. (Leviticus 17:11, 14 KJV)

Notice the distinctions related to blood. The human physical body has flesh and blood, but notice as the resurrected Jesus speaks...

Look at my hands and my feet. It is I myself! Touch me and see; a ghost does not have flesh and bones, as you see I have." (Luke 24:39)

The resurrected body has flesh and bone (no blood). The phrase 'flesh and blood' is a common term used in both the Old and New Testaments (21 times). The fact that Luke (a doctor) notes Jesus' use of the term 'flesh and bone' has to be taken as significant. Apparently a resurrected, glorified body, while still using the same term 'flesh', has a much different physical biology (if we can use that word).

It is clear we see two distinct species here; two eternal identities. Some (the RULERS) will be set-apart from the human species; and will cease to be human as we know it today. This is reinforced by Scripture:

I declare to you, brothers and sisters, that flesh and blood cannot inherit the kingdom of God, nor does the perishable inherit the imperishable. (I Corinthians 15:50)

RULERS have their existence rooted in the life of God, perhaps even outside of time. But how do the CITIZENS, who are not immortal, live eternally?

Eternal Life

Once again, the answer appears to start back in Genesis. Two special trees were in the midst of the garden. One was the tree of life. After Adam sinned, he and Eve were banished from the garden and the tree of life.

> And the LORD God said, "The man has now become like one of us, knowing good and evil. He must not be allowed to reach out his hand and take also from the tree of life and eat, and live forever." (Genesis 3:22)
>
> After he drove the man out, he placed on the east side of the Garden of Eden cherubim and a flaming sword flashing back and forth to guard the way to the tree of life. (Genesis 3:24)

It seems apparent that Adam was not immortal. It was intended that he and his descendants should live forever by eating of the tree of life. When he sinned, eternal life was denied him by denying access to the tree of life.

The tree of life does not appear again until the end of the Millennium. Apparently even during the 1000-year Millennium humans (sheep, CITIZENS) may die at an old age.

But then…

> And I saw a new heaven and a new earth: for the first heaven and the first earth were passed away; and there was no more sea. And I John saw the holy city, new Jerusalem, coming down from God out of heaven, prepared as a bride adorned for her husband. (Revelation 21:1-2 KJV)

… and the tree of life…

> And he shewed me a pure river of water of life, clear as crystal, proceeding out of the throne of God and of the Lamb. In the midst of the street of it, and on either side of the river, [was

there] the tree of life, which bare twelve [manner of] fruits, [and]
yielded her fruit every month: and the leaves of the tree [were]
for the healing of the nations. (Revelation 22:1-2 KJV)

The tree is back, and available, *'for the healing of the nations'*.

The holy city, prepared as a bride, quite evidently represents the RULERS. Out of the city flows the river that supports the trees of life that heals the nations. The imagery seems clear; the life of the Lamb and the Bride (RULERS) together, empower and sustain 'eternal life' for the CITIZENS.

The adults of heaven, king and queen as 'parents', will bless the children of the universe with life, forever. We will see how true this is as we look at our last distinction–reproduction.

Reproduction

The last distinction we will look at is reproduction. It appears, as we said earlier, that the RULERS are 'corporately complete' at the resurrection (perhaps even at the 'revealing'). There is marriage, but no marrying (new marriages with children), in heaven.

Now then, at the resurrection whose wife will she be, since the
seven were married to her?" Jesus replied, "The people of this
age marry and are given in marriage. But those who are
considered worthy of taking part in that age and in the
resurrection from the dead will neither marry nor be given in
marriage, and they can no longer die; for they are like the
angels. They are God's children, since they are children of the
resurrection. (Luke 20:33-36)

This people group, the RULERS, are no longer part of human society. They are one with Messiah, expressing his life as his bride, a priesthood, etc., adopted into the family of God, to manage creation (earth). They may live among humans, but after the resurrection they cease being flesh and blood humans. They do not reproduce; their numbers will never increase. Now, God's Son has a bride, the divine family is complete. Except...for the children.

God's nature is fruitfulness; ever growing and expanding. Unlike the RULERS, the CITIZENS as a group, will expand forever.

Yes, there are 'children', spiritual, human children. Notice this verse from Hebrews (quoting Isaiah 8:18).

> And again, "I will put my trust in him." And again he says, "Here am I, _and the children God has given me_." Since _the children have flesh and blood_, he too shared in their humanity so that by his death he might break the power of him who holds the power of death--that is, the devil (Hebrews 2:13-14)

The humans (CITIZENS) will expand forever. Someday the universe will be full of flesh and blood humans (managed by the RULERS). Notice this passage about the 'increase of [his] government'.

> For unto us a child is born, unto us a son is given: and the government shall be upon his shoulder: and his name shall be called Wonderful, Counsellor, The mighty God, The everlasting Father, The Prince of Peace. _Of the increase of [his] government and peace [there shall be] no end_, upon the throne of David, and upon his kingdom, to order it, and to establish it with judgment and with justice from henceforth even for ever. The zeal of the LORD of hosts will perform this. (Isaiah 9:6-7 KJV)

We have spent some effort looking at the detailed bodily characteristics of the two eternal living people groups. It helps to make them more real, and less abstract.

From body type details, we now need to zoom out to see more details of the actual resurrections, the process of how one qualifies to be part of a group. And lastly, we will look at judges and the judgement process.

Two Mass Resurrections

As of this writing, the world has not seen a 'mass resurrection'. While we do have, in our past, isolated examples of both types of 'raisings', resuscitation and resurrection, the Bible only refers to two mass resurrections in the future (or one mass resurrection and one mass resuscitation in our terms).

One is associated with the beginning of the millennium (resurrection) and one is associated with the end of the millennium (resuscitation). It's important to note that other than these two mass 'resurrections' there does not appear to be random or selective individual or mass 'resurrections' at other times.

The First Mass Resurrection

The first mass resurrection, the one closely associated with the timing of the Sheep and the Goats Parable, near the beginning of the Millennium, is a special resurrection of the sons of God (RULERS). This is the event that all true Christians look forward to, often called the rapture. We have, as the model, the individual resurrection of Messiah Jesus' to look back upon and observe.

It is a resurrection of the living and the dead. Ironically, according to Christian theology (and rightly so), many of those resurrected are Old Testament saints closely associated with Judaism, who believed in the Messiah, yet never heard of Jesus (the Messiah) in their lifetime. Candidates (among many others) would be, Adam, Noah, Abraham, Joseph, Moses, Joshua, Elisha, David, (and the women of course), etc.

Apparently, the ministry of Jesus and the salvation he offers (RULERS), via the work of the Holy Spirit, is retroactive. A knowledgeable faith and hope in the Messiah previous to the coming of the literal Messiah, qualified one to be part of the Messiah's work. This is not some Twentieth Century Christian revisionist history trying to claim Jewish Patriarchs for its own. No, Christian theology (ideally)

234 · THE SHEEP AND THE GOATS PARABLE

comes from the Jewish writers of the New Testament. (It has strayed a bit over the millennia but that will be corrected.)

The first (special) resurrection is described by Jewish writers of the New Testament. It is their idea, born from their scripture and their traditions. Christians accept this as the Word of God, and rightly so. They have given us the theology of the resurrection, and even, as in the Book of Hebrews, named names. Hebrews 11 gives us the Hall of Faith with numerous Old Testament names. Hebrews develops the essential idea of 'perfection' and links it with something it calls 'the promise'.

Perfection is a complex issue that even Christianity has not come to terms with, but Hebrews says (in so many words) it is part of 'the promise' given to Israel. We introduced the subject of perfection back in Chapter 10 and will not add more to that heated and complex discussion here, but (prophetic) 'sinless perfection' is absolutely an essential component of the Restoration we have been talking about.

Hebrews connects the resurrection with the promise...

For yet a little while, and he that shall come will come, and will not tarry. (Hebrews 10:37 KJV)

...and then states that the work of Messiah transcends both old and new covenants (the original and re-newed covenant). This work must be realized in the Restoration BEFORE the resurrection can take place. Back to Hebrews...

And these all, having obtained a good report through faith, received not the promise: God having provided some better thing for us, that they without us should not be made perfect. (Hebrews 11:39-40 KJV)

The first resurrection is a 'special resurrection', or as Paul calls it, the 'out-resurrection', which is clearly distinguished from the second, or 'general resurrection' at the end of the Millennium. Note these Scriptures about the first:

If by any means I might attain unto the resurrection [Greek, out-resurrection, exanastasis] of the dead. (Philippians 3:11).

And I saw thrones, and they sat upon them, and judgment was given unto them: ... and they lived and reigned with Christ a thousand years. But the rest of the dead lived not again until the thousand years were finished. This [is] the first resurrection (anastasis). Blessed and holy [is] he that hath part in the first resurrection: on such the second death hath no power, but they shall be priests of God and of Christ, and shall reign with him a thousand years. (Revelation 20:4-6 KJV)

Women received back their dead, raised to life again (resuscitated). Others were tortured and refused to be released, so that they might gain a better resurrection. (Hebrews 11:35)

This is the resurrection Paul hopes to 'attain' too. These three terms, 'out-resurrection', 'first resurrection', and 'better resurrection' refer to the same mass resurrection.

This resurrection is for the 'priests of God and of Christ', those who will rule and reign for a thousand years. Together with Christ, and under his authority, both Old Testament and post Calvary saints (RULERS) are God's management priesthood of the universe. This is where we get our term for one of the people groups—the RULERS.

The Final General Mass Resuscitation

But there is also a final general mass 'raising' (resuscitation) that we mentioned earlier from Daniel:

Multitudes who sleep in the dust of the earth will awake: some to everlasting life, others to shame and everlasting contempt. (Daniel 12:2)

This is the final dissolution of all mankind, living and dead (excluding the RULERS). Perhaps it could be thought of as 'The Sheep and Goats II' (except the original parable at the beginning of the Millennium deals only with the living). But it is towards the same end—who will be the CITIZENS who propagate the new world to come (first the Millennium, then the new heavens and new earth).

Notice the design here. There is a judicial process at the beginning of the Millennium to eliminate the REBELS, and there is a judicial process at the end of the Millennium to eliminate the REBLES. Who are left? In both cases, the people left alive to populate the earth are 'sheep', or CITIZENS in our terminology.

Since the first resurrection there have been two parallel tracks in God's program. The judicial processes above are directed exclusively at flesh and blood humans (CITIZENS and REBELS), not RULERS. The RULERS were exclusively and permanently set-aside and 'corporately complete' at the first resurrection.

Take note—there is one, and only one, glorified resurrection. Since that point, the RULERS have been part of 'management' (ruling and reigning). No humans after the first resurrection will ever become glorified RULERS (unless God were to make an exception we are not aware of). The 'sheep', whether at the beginning or the end of the millennium, DO NOT become RULERS when it's all over.

So, we could summarize the mass resurrections as such: the first finalizes the RULERS, and the second finalizes the CITIZENS. And finally, the REBELS, and demonic forces and angels are eliminated from the living universe.

First Summary

The implications of these ideas are prophetically shocking from a traditional Christian theology perspective. In this parable once again, we see evidence of the three people groups in God's eternal design. Two of them 'live' forever, the third exists forever (the second death). This implies there are two types of 'salvation' (living forever). Of the faithful, some are 'saved by the blood' onto perfect works, and some are saved by faithful good works (note the Sheep and Goats Parable).

The Sheep and Goats Parable lock-in this idea. It is interesting that it is the final parable of Jesus' ministry. The idea that there are two eternal people groups was eluded to from the first verse of the Bible, *'In the beginning God created the heavens and the earth'*. That is to say, there are heavenly people and there are earthly people. As that thread continues to run through the Bible, we see the two priesthoods, we see Abraham's two mothers of his two sons, etc., etc., as noted earlier.

This truth has not been needed for Godly living or salvation. But it is needed for 'all-truth' and the prophetic program the RULERS (we) are about to orchestrate. Long before the first resurrection, the 'sons' are revealed and prepared, and take on management of the 'business'. More and more, 'man' is managing his own creative week, clearly modeled after 'week one' of Genesis.

What is the purpose of this long, tumultuous 7000-year 'week'? Well, through childhood and beyond, it is primarily to test and divide mankind. Within the scope of God's sovereign purposes, each man has chosen his path, worked out his own salvation, and determined his eternal destiny. Adam's descendants have split into three streams (not two).

One group, with an eternally fixed number of people, become part of the divine family; the other group will be forever expanding, eventually filling the 'new heavens and new earth' universe. Each have their function and jurisdiction in maintaining a holy, glorious, righteous, and fruitful paradise forever.

The Sheep and Goats Parable is a remarkable end to Jesus' prophetic survey in Matthew 24 and 25. Honestly understood, it disrupts the current 'heaven or hell' Christian theology and any prophetic model built around it. We see a new people group, a new 'salvation' and a new responsibility for those truly 'in Christ'.

The coming of the kingdom to earth requires the functioning of both RULERS and CITIZENS in their proper roles. It must become clear to Christianity that its greatest priority is '*the kingdom*', and '*God's will being done on earth as it is in heaven*', not 'going to heaven'. We remember Jesus' words, '*seek first the kingdom...*' (Matthew 6:33).

A Prophetic Priority—Feed My Sheep

An interesting question is, who are the sheep? One is reminded of Jesus' words to Peter after Jesus' resurrection. Three times Jesus admonished Peter to 'feed my sheep (lambs)'. Most teachers will read that and hear Jesus emphasizing the need to 'preach the Word'. As true and important as that is, prophetically, it goes far beyond 'spiritual food and care'. Jesus is charging RULERS, through Peter, with their fundamental responsibility to prepare a kingdom of righteousness, peace, and joy through the **Restoration** of creation. And more directly, to recreate a kingdom paradise on earth for the benefit of the sheep (CITIZENS).

Before we end this rather technical exposition of the Sheep and Goats Parable and resurrections, let's look at three more related issues: 1) contrasting the selection process of CITIZENS and RULERS, 2) exercising judgement, and 3) group rewards.

Contrasting the Selection Process of CITIZENS and RULERS

As noted above, there is a judicial process at both the beginning of the millennium and the end of the millennium to determine who are CITIZENS. The first resurrection (which identifies the RULERS) on the other hand, is sudden and decisive. We see no judicial process preceding or following the resurrection (or rapture).

In light of the Sheep and Goats event, which happens just a few days later, why is it that the sheep have a formal judicial process separating them from the goats, but the RULERS are instantly, in the blink of an eye, identified and separated from those 'left behind', with no judicial process? We may wonder, why is there this different treatment of the groups?

Selecting RULERS

The reason we see no judicial process connected with the first resurrection is because the 'sons' were 'revealed' decades before the resurrection and they have been being refined ever since. There was a judicial process at the 'revealing'. The whole world had the ultimate judicial process given to them. Note the first commission:

> *And this gospel of the kingdom will be preached in the whole world as a testimony to all nations, and then the end will come. (Matthew 24:14)*

The *'gospel-of-the-kingdom'*, was given as a *'testimony to all nations'*. This is a legal proceeding. As we said earlier, 'this gospel', spoken with massive miraculous power and signs, was given to the whole world. Given this testimony, unlike anything the world had ever seen, people made their decisions, and then 'the end'.

'The end' is the end of the human option to become Sons of God. The end result of this event is what Paul calls, *'the revealing of the sons of God'* (Romans 8:19). Those who will be resurrected decades later were largely determined at 'the end'. Another view of this decision event is revealed in the parable of the 'Wheat and the Tares'.

So, in fact, the resurrection does have a judicial-type process, except it was initiated decades earlier. Why this long interval, we might ask? Because the 'sons' (RULERS) had to be identified and 'leave the world' (go into the wilderness) to begin their training for their final perfection and ministry, long before their resurrection. The RULERS must be identified, restored, and perfected in a generation-long process BEFORE they are immortalized. For the RULERS, the issue of obedience must be firmly settled BEFORE resurrection. Because of this long testing period, when the time comes for the first resurrection, it can happen 'in the blink of an eye'.

The sheep (CITIZENS), on the other hand, are not immortal or necessarily expected to be perfect. Therefore, they can be judged on a less rigorous basis and welcomed into the refinement of the Millennium process.

Exercising Judgement—Royal Judges

The Sheep and Goats Parable implicitly gives us one more insight into the RULERS' responsibility. As we said, at the time of the events of the parable the RULERS have already been resurrected. They are not directly mentioned in the parable but nonetheless, they are present. Jesus, sometime earlier, had revealed what the RULERS would be doing at this event. Note this Scripture:

> *Jesus said to them, "Truly I tell you, at the renewal of all things, when the Son of Man sits on his glorious throne, you who have followed me will also sit on twelve thrones, judging the twelve tribes of Israel." (Matthew 19:28)*

And reiterating the Sheep and Goats Parable:

> *"When the Son of Man comes in his glory, and all the angels with him, he will sit on his glorious throne. All the nations will be gathered before him, and he will separate the people one from another as a shepherd separates the sheep from the goats." (Matthew 25:31-32)*

The identical phrase 'when the Son of Man ... sits on his glorious throne' from both passages, and the virtually identical context would indicate both scriptures are pointing at the same event. It is the judgement of the nations, including Israel. One passage mentions the twelve tribes and one mentions the nations. Of the lot, some are judged to be CITIZENS and some are REBELS. Judging and separating the two groups is the purpose of this event.

Specifically, it says the twelve (Apostles, who are RULERS) will judge the twelve tribes. It is likely then, that other RULERS will also judge the nations. At a symbolic level, the 'twelve tribes of Israel' are representative of the nations of earth—the CITIZENS. And the twelve Apostles are representative of all of the royal judges—the RULERS.

We need to note that it is likely that the primary role of the RULERS, forever, is to be judges. When we use the term RULERS, it is not in the sense of the current world system. Kingdom RULERS do not lord it over the CITIZENS by demanding privilege and wealth for themselves. No, the RULERS effectively manage the top-level judicial system of the universe.

In the kingdom, which is a highly legal administration, the CITIZENS will have their own courts and judges, but there are times that higher authorities will have to weigh in. The RULERS essentially serve the CITIZENS by maintaining righteousness and justice (and discipline) when needed.

The Sheep and Goats Parable indicates this 'judging' role begins for the RULERS right out of the resurrection gate. So, what is there to judge? Whether the people have accepted Jesus as their savior and Messiah? No! There has been no 'Jesus salvation' for many decades at this point. (Many may certainly believe that Jesus is the savior, and that he is the Jewish Messiah, but that does not make one a RULERS at this point. That privileged salvation ended with the 'end' of the world, and the 'Last Passover', decades before (as we described earlier).

You are a 'saved' CITIZEN (sheep) if you have lived righteously. Specifically, in this case, the testimony revolves around your treatment of 'the least of these my brethren'. It might be how the righteous of the nations treated the Jews (Israelites) during their time of persecution. The bottom line is, at this time, faithful righteous behavior (even under extreme conditions) is what saves you.

But the main issue we are trying to make here is the judicial process itself, not so much the detailed judicial arguments. Rather, who are the judges? There is widespread perception that God or Jesus are the judges of mankind, the only judges, because, 'they are God', or 'only they know the thoughts of man'.

It must be conceded that in an ultimate sense, there is some truth to this. However, in a practical sense, the responsibility needs to swing to the human side. We are nearing a time, prophetically, when we could say, no, it is men who will judge men. That is a primary role of the RULERS.

In our sheep parable, 'the King' is the presiding judge. Of course, everyone assumes that is Jesus, as he 'sits on his glorious throne'. But associated verses also say, 'the twelve' will judge.

We don't have to get extremely dogmatic here, and there is room for debate, but the premise can be asserted that it will be man who will make even 'earth or hell' judgements, overseen by the ultimate judge.

Let's review a few Scriptures that might point us in that direction. First...

> *For the Father judgeth no man, but hath committed all judgment unto the Son: ... I can of mine own self do nothing: as I hear, I judge: and my judgment is just; because I seek not mine own will, but the will of the Father which hath sent me. (John 5:22, 30 KJV)*

Why shouldn't the Father judge; who would be better? But there is an important principle here. As man matures and the prophetic purposes are fulfilled, judgement is moving downstream, closer to the defendants. In God's mind, this appears to be righteous.

The RULERS are now part of the divine team (conformed to the image of the Son). It seems apparent that they are the ones who will be making the judgements, dividing the sheep and the goats. Jesus is the head judge; he certainly presides over the preceding and affirms the final judgement, but we should note this larger issue of who judges. John says this of Jesus:

For God sent not his Son into the world to condemn the world; but that the world through him might be saved. (John 3:17 KJV)

And these other snippets:

The men of Nineveh will stand up at the judgment with this generation and condemn it;... (Matthew 12:41 KJV)

The Queen of the South will rise at the judgment with this generation and condemn it;... (Matthew 12:42 KJV)

By faith Noah, ... condemned the world,... (Hebrews 11:7 KJV)

Or do you not know that the Lord's people will judge the world? And if you are to judge the world, are you not competent to judge trivial cases? Do you not know that we will judge angels? How much more the things of this life! (I Corinthians 6:2-3)

In America, we have this concept of a 'jury of one's peers'. The divine Word became flesh and dwelt among us. His function was primarily 'salvation' (in the fullest sense). He was tempted, but never sinned. He was full of the Holy Ghost power from birth. He has some distinctions that no other man can claim.

A good lawyer might be able to convince the judge (and jury) that Jesus cannot relate to 'sinful' man since he was never sinful. Therefore, he is not qualified to 'condemn' mankind. There is an argument here, and Scripture seems to support the idea of (regular or former) men condemning other men. It is likely that it will be the RULERS who make up, at minimum, the lowest (heavenly) judicial courts. It is likely they, who will weigh the evidence and make an initial ruling, with Jesus then affirming their ruling.

To close this section on the sheep and the goats, and how that parable supports two people groups, let's deal with one last issue—rewards.

Rewards—Inherit the kingdom prepared for you from the foundation of the world

Once identified properly, we notice that the sheep (CITIZENS) were not resurrected, nor will they ever be resurrected. Their reward is what mankind was promised from the beginning, a paradise on earth, their own garden, and eternal human life, (assuming they remain 'sheep', of course). We know that by the end of the millennium some of these sheep (or their children) turn out to be REBELS (Revelation 20).

Notice the earthly reward of the sheep:

> *Then shall the King say unto them on his right hand, Come, ye blessed of my Father, inherit the kingdom prepared for you from the foundation of the world: (Matthew 25:34 KJV)*

This is CITIZEN salvation, with CITIZEN reward not a resurrection. It is a return to the paradise exemplified by the Garden of Eden. The kingdom here is the 'heaven on earth' kingdom. It is for the nations of earth, peace, prosperity, and their own garden; and for Israel, the Royal House of David to inherit all its promises. Here is one for Israel…

> *"The days are coming," declares the LORD, "when the reaper will be overtaken by the plowman and the planter by the one treading grapes. New wine will drip from the mountains and flow from all the hills, and I will bring my people Israel back from exile. "They will rebuild the ruined cities and live in them. They will plant vineyards and drink their wine; they will make gardens and eat their fruit. I will plant Israel in their own land, never again to be uprooted from the land I have given them," says the LORD your God. (Amos 9:13-15)*

The parable's sheep are welcomed into the extended blessings of natural Israel. The parable indicates that all the promises to 'earthly' Israel will be fulfilled. Israel will be the first nation of earth and the nations will come up to Zion to learn the ways of the Lord. All CITIZENS, both Israel and the nations, are the recipients of the spiritual and physical inheritance intended for mankind.

Rewards—Come and Share Your Master's Happiness!

However, notice the contrast between the sheep (CITIZENS) reward above and the reward given to the faithful servants (RULERS) in the second parable of Matthew 25, The Parable of the Talents.

> *"His master replied, 'Well done, good and faithful servant! You have been faithful with a few things; I will put you in charge of many things. Come and share your master's happiness!'" (Matthew 25:23)*

For the RULERS, their reward is less material and more intimate. They will be 'in charge' and 'share their master's happiness'. For the RULERS, their inheritance is a relationship and a responsibility, not directly a piece of the material creation. They will eventually engage mankind as a 'holy city' made without hands. Their eternal responsibility is to care for and oversee the well-being of the 'sheep'.

Chapter Conclusion

This aspect of taking major responsibility for the material world, and the kingdom on earth, (before the second Coming) is a major blind spot in current Christian prophecy. In Adam's day, he was told to take dominion over the fish, the birds, and the animals. But that limited responsibility expanded after the 'fall'. The RULERS today, 'sitting in heavenly places' and native 'citizens' of heaven, are looking down on a new and serious responsibility to prepare this world and its people for the coming King.

Ultimately, the intent of this book is to bring us to understand that God expects man to apprehend reality and to express that reality in a tangible kingdom on earth. That is what sparks the *Restoration*, the sons being ready to resume their responsibility. That responsibility first requires an internal 'renewing of the mind'. Truth is the active-ingredient and the leading indicator of that transformation.

A remnant (initially) of Christianity who seek out the truth, will become 'the prophet' (or spirit of the prophet) mentioned earlier and lead in this final and essential *Restoration*. We have an opportunity here, in Jesus' last parable, to confront our own concept of reality against his words. These words matter. God will mightily use those few people who will struggle past the singular goal of 'salvation', onto the ultimate quest of discovering reality.

Chapter Fourteen

CONCLUSION - A PROPHETIC CHALLENGE:

If there is one word that summarizes the prophecy model described in this book it is (adult) RESPONSIBILITY, and a second would be VICTORY.

The story begins in Genesis. There we are given a reference to God's intentions, a garden paradise on earth and a beautiful family. But now we know that the first dream was for showing intent only. It wasn't to last.

In the 'fall', mankind would, like God, begin HIS 'week' of creating; creating a permanent world. As in all human childhoods, our loving parent would provide all things necessary for godliness; the full spectrum of eternal gifts and callings placed within man. They would slowly be expressed outwardly from within the body of mankind, some for noble use, some for common, and some for wrath.

Finishing his 'week' of **hard service** (childhood), 'the end' will come and mankind's Sabbath (millennium) will begin. The 'adult sons' are revealed as managers of the 'first generation'. By restoring the new world to 'first principles', it will empower the three distinct 'species' of mankind the opportunity to emerge and excel as RULERS, CITIZENS, or REBELS.

Each calling will grow to maturity; some to immortal God-likeness, some to paradise on earth, and some to satanic-damnation. In struggle and pain, God's full intent for mankind would be advanced and perfected. The first Adam was conflicted. He had three identities within him, therefore he fell. They too, like Eve, needed to be 'revealed'. When that is done, 'man' will be victorious; the kingdom will come; God's will on earth will be done. True '*Adam*' will soon, once again, be tending the garden, and the King of the universe (Messiah) will come.

Short-circuiting our RESPONSIBILITY as servant rulers is perverse. An undue focus on 'going to heaven' has produced defective prophecy and an ill prepared church. A worldview focused on REWARD and not RESPONSIBILITY, continues the sin of Adam.

The summary above is discordant with current Christian eschatology, in both process and outcome. Current prophecy does not emphasize 'a return to the Garden' RESPONSIBILITY, nor does it envision any meaningful human VICTORY in character or dominion this side of resurrection. Remember, resurrection is a diploma not a rescue!

Judge for yourself. Having read 'The Prophetic Story of Mankind' in this book, can you accept that it is an extremely viable account of 'how the kingdom comes' to earth.

If so, is it time to consider a new prophecy model; a new prophetic story? Ultimately, prophecy is not a curiosity or an academic exercise. It is also not about survival or evangelism, although these can be welcome by-products. Prophecy is intimacy with God. It is an exercise in separating illusion from reality. Prophecy is the pathway to all-truth, the heritage and glory of the sons of God.

It is the spiritual and political solution to the painful experiment of a fallen human earth. We are responsible to exercise this gift of truth-seeking by piecing together those secrets God has revealed to us. Like the servants working with 'talents', we multiply what we have been given until we connect the dots, and fill-in the blanks, line upon line, precept upon precept.

These lofty goals require effort and sacrifice. We must give priority and time to study and thought. And like Abraham, we must (at minimum metaphorically) be willing to leave our family, traditions, and comfort-zones, and travel to a foreign place.

This may sound unnecessarily philosophical and extreme for many. After all, it's only prophecy. Our teachers tell us prophecy is not essential doctrine; it's optional. You can believe virtually anything about prophecy, or nothing, and yet be a Christian in good standing, they say. Perhaps, in a practical sense today, that is largely true. But this half-truth stems from Christianity's heaven and hell worldview. By clinging to this view, the only real measurable goal in life is to get into heaven, and, they say, your prophecy model (or not) has no connection to being 'saved'. But this half-truth will eventually prove to be dangerous.

The Christian walk cannot be isolated from its prophetic end. Nature tells us the end may be what is most important; it's 'the harvest'. What is a wheat field if it does not produce fruit? Parables like 'The Wheat and Tares', 'The Wise and Foolish Virgins', and many living Biblical examples, remind us that falsity may exist, whilst we remain dangerously unaware. The end often reveals who we really are. End-time prophecy is designed to test one's reality. True faith must be directed toward true promises.

The Prophetic Spark

As we explained earlier about the prophetic season, the stage has been set. It's sundown, the end of the work-week. You must be aware that the rules change on Friday evening? It's Sabbath!

Again, our Christian teachers tell us Sabbath rules are obsolete. Christian theology has largely been stripped of these 'obsolete' concepts, and likewise so has Christian prophecy.

What do you think? Will God use Biblical patterns such as Sabbath and Passover to build the new world (kingdom)? Do the rules change Friday night? Choose your prophetic model carefully; much is at stake.

Just as David's permanent Temple was not conceived via command, the permanent kingdom (new world) will be born out of the faithful's response.

On the prophetic stage, it's Friday eve; the sons have reached the time of their Bar Mitzvah (near adulthood); the Sabbath is about to begin. It will only take a spark—the prophet. As he walks on stage, the program begins. The main plot is...not the Rapture, but the *Restoration*!

The spark of the *Restoration* is the rebirth of the prophetic ministry, in the Spirit of *Elijah*. The author of this essay is not aware of any prophet on earth today, much less, 'the prophet', '*Elijah*'. *Elijah* (a single person, or a small team, makes no difference), is the director of the first commission (Matthew 24:14). This initial message to the world will be the 'gospel-of-the-kingdom'—a worldwide, enforced introduction to kingdom culture via the Passover, and very likely the shock and awe that comes with it.

Elijah's first task is to engage his fellow Saints (Christianity). First, a larger group of prophetic ministers who will prophetically equip an even much larger evangelistic pastoral body.

The details of this commission and this complex (largely unknown) gospel will be covered in more depth later. Our intent here is to give enough detail to allow one to contrast it with other prophetic models— the present JUDGEMENT centric models, and a true RESPONSIBILITY (VICTORY) model, and to show how unprepared most people will be when confronted with these adult choices.

Mankind's problem from the Garden is not just 'sin and death', it is our judgment of reality. That's why Paul talks about 'renewing the mind' (Romans 12:2) and Jesus says, '*the truth* will set us free' (John 8:32). In our childhood, we have come to believe 'getting saved' is the goal. No, getting saved is the means, truth is the goal, and resurrection is the final diploma. Truth is our responsibility and our heritage.

An 'Uber-Guardian' Again

Why is this so important to understand? Looking back at the Garden, we see Adam as a sort of uber-guardian of the universe. When he fell, the universe fell with him into chaos. This is why Paul tells us:

> *The [whole] creation waits in eager expectation for the sons of God to be revealed. (Romans 8:19)*

Why? Because once revealed (as adult sons) the creation will have its uber-guardian once again. God can relax the 'chaos', and through the merit of the sons, the creation will once again be blessed and at peace. (At least the first release; the last release, death, will come at the end of the Millennium.)

This is a great mystery, and it has been given virtually no consideration in today's Christian prophecy, except to relegate it, a kingdom paradise, to a post resurrection, God only knows, event (essentially a fantasy).

Interestingly, this mysterious concept of the uber-guardian role played by **Adam** may be confirmed by science.

Theories developed recently in the field of quantum mechanics seem to point to the possibility of an object (a universe or part of the universe) being in multiple (perhaps infinite) states, all at the same time. We could see how this multiple-realities, all at the same time, might correlate to a state of chaos or truth-lessness. It could correspond to the current state of chaos after the fall.

The science gets even more bizarre when they discovered that when there is a 'super-observer' (someone observing a quantum setting), the object reverts to a single state. When the super-observer is not looking it reverts to multiple states; when the super-observer is observing again it returns to a single state.

In effect, when a super-observer is observing a setting, that setting is transformed from multiple-states (chaos) to a single state (truth).

Whether or not quantum mechanics is actually the scientific theory behind the state of the universe before and after the curse, it helps to illustrate how the spiritual reality may work. It also helps to give much greater relevance to Paul's comment '*the whole creation is waiting for the revealing of the sons of God*', and Jesus's references to '*the truth setting us free*' and '*the Spirit leading us into all-truth*'.

Yes, the whole creation is waiting for the super-observer or the uber-guardian (*Adam*) to resume his responsibility originally given in the Garden. All-truth, reality as God sees it, is an essential achievement of the sons of God because reality is actually defined and maintained in the universe by these sons. For the CITIZENS (the people of creation), their reality is defined and maintained by the RULERS.

This is why the *Restoration* is so important. The RULERS will undertake to create a new world according to their reality, as explained earlier. Creating a born-again world is their final exam before resurrection and immortality. There must be absolute certainty of perfection (no deformities) BEFORE the sons of God are immortalized (resurrected).

The Spirit of God has been nurturing those sons for the last 2000 years. God is waiting for evidence that they have truly overcome their corruption and are ready for adult service. Deciphering the Millennium commissions and writing a blueprint of a new born-again world in sync with the Fathers will, is that evidence.

Faithful Judaism has been setting a place for Elijah for much of 2000 years. They send a child to the door to look for him each Passover. Some Passover soon, God will decide it is finally his time. Mankind has given evidence they can truly '*prepare the way for the Lord*'. It will be done of course, and surely, we will hear, "*Well done, good and faithful servants*".

Pray for the coming of *Elijah*.

One Question: A Personal-Discovery Exercise

One Question!

...to Discover the Millennium Commissions

This Appendix is an optional personal-discovery exercise. Some people like to discover things for themselves. If that's you—you can! The full prophecy model of this book is centered on elements from Jesus' prophetic sermon in Mathew 24. But, remarkably, the real structure and most relevant portions of that sermon have not been identified, nor will they be found in any Christian commentary. (More evidence for the need of prophetic reformation). How could our scholars and teachers have missed this? Answer this question for yourself.

But, even if you don't want to do the exercise in full, you should read through it as an introduction to this critical foundation.

And we welcome your comments.

Introduction and Instructions

Please:

This exercise was intended to be straightforward: Read Matthew 24 carefully and answer the question as requested. This is a solemn prophetic exercise, which leads to very serious implications. Please do not take it casually. Proceed only if you can come to 'rest' and take the necessary time (at least 30 minutes) to read the necessary passage, think and meditate upon the specified issues.

Introduction:

When Jesus charged his followers to 'seek first the kingdom...,' he was identifying the only pathway to a new and glorious world. He was saying that the solution to the world's needs and problems is found in the prophetic kingdom. This kingdom concept and how it actually comes, or is manifested on earth, is poorly understood. There are numerous, radically diverse opinions on the end-times, but none offer a detailed scenario on how God's will is done on earth. Why are there such differing and inadequate opinions? Is this confusion justified? Did God intend for man to understand the end-of-the-age and the transition to the kingdom?

These are all good questions without easy answers. But there is one question that will bring unprecedented new clarity to the end-of-the-age discussion. The answer to this question will provide a kind of 'missing-link' to end-of-the-age prophecy. Amazingly, this hidden doorway has been right before our eyes for 2000 years. It comes from the very words of Jesus in perhaps the most studied prophecy chapter in the Bible. If true, it will bring an unparalleled shift in prophetic understanding. Ponder the magnitude of this; an end-of-the-age breakthrough, discovered just in time for the end-of-the-age. It's as if this was God's intention all along!

Instructions

To unfold this question properly, it has been laid out in the two sections described below.

The Question

The first section is the question itself. Follow the instructions and do the exercise. Answer the question in the space on the bottom without looking at 'The Short Answer' section on the following pages. Review the definitions if necessary.

The Short Answer and Summary

The second section is a summary explanation. It is a short, three to four page statement of the 'answer' with specific verses and a short-paraphrased summary of those verses revealing Jesus' effective meaning. Whether one does the exercise or not, be sure to read the Short Answer.

Background

Based on the New Testament, Jesus delivered only one comprehensive prophecy message that contains a panorama of prophetic 'last days' events. Scholars have named this message the 'Olivet Discourse' and the most complete record of it is found in Matthew 24-25 (also Mark 13 & Luke 21).

Definitions: (Of words found in 'The Question')

Commission: a prophetic worldwide positive offensive (a strategic event that is assigned a limited time to start and end), whether it be in the form of a message alone or with strategic actions. A commission is neither a general command, nor a directive regarding warnings or issues of righteous behavior.

For example: Christianity as a whole has taken from Jesus' words in Matthew 28:19 one worldwide corporate assignment that has come to be called 'the Great Commission'. "Therefore, go and make disciples of all nations, baptizing them in the name of the Father and of the Son and of the Holy Spirit..." This an example of a commission given to followers of Jesus. However, for our purposes, it is NOT a prophetic commission because it did not have a limited duration, thus far, being in continuous operation for 2000 years.

Minister: someone mature, competent and knowledgeable in Scripture and active service, not just a believer or worshiper of God.

Followers: dedicated members of the worldwide 'body of Messiah.' (professing true Christians with a prophetic anointing).

The Question:

Read Matthew 24 quietly and meditatively, with the attitude of a minister. Look for one specific type of instruction – a commission.

You are not looking for warnings, admonitions, or statements, but a commission (see definitions on previous page).

While reading this chapter, can you identify one or more commissions Jesus assigned to his followers in this panoramic presentation of 'last days' events?

In simple terms: What critically important project or projects is Jesus commissioning his people to do at the end-of-the-age?

Answers:

One or more Commissions found, include verse #

: _____

: _____

: _____

The Short Answer

Jesus gave us only one prophecy message where he surveyed the entire end-of-the-age (Matthew 24-25). And although it is somewhat implicit in this message, there are clearly two commissions revealed by Jesus. The commissions will be carried out by his faithful followers at the appointed times. The two commissions are in Chapter 24, verses 14 and 45. Below, both commissions are listed with the original (implicit) wording followed by a paraphrased (explicit) translation. Also, notice the added 'interval' which may not be considered a commission, but is nevertheless a vital 'assignment' which is a critical part of the 'two commissions'.

Definitions:

Implicit: Implied though not plainly expressed.

Explicit: Stated clearly and in detail, leaving no room for confusion or doubt.

First Commission: Verse 14

Original (Implicit): "And this gospel-of-the-kingdom will be preached in the whole world as a testimony to all nations, and then the end will come."

Paraphrase (Explicit): "And you, my disciples, will 'preach' an unprecedented gospel of truth and power as a testimony of the one true God to all nations, and then the 'world as we know it' will end, and the kingdom world will begin."

Second Commission: Verse 45

Original (Implicit): "Who then is the faithful and wise servant, whom the master has put in charge of the servants in his household to give them their food at the proper time?"

Paraphrase (Explicit): As the first set-apart kingdom generation perfected in my likeness, you, my disciples, will be my faithful and wise servants, whom I will put in charge of earth's 'citizens' to bring them under the covenant by selling them food during the great (Sabbath) famine, as prefigured in the story of Joseph (and Jesus' own 'feeding' miracles)."

The Interval (between commissions): Verse 34

Original (Implicit): "I tell you the truth, this generation will certainly not pass away until all these things have happened."

Paraphrase (Explicit): "I tell you the truth, this newborn wilderness generation, set apart from the world (by the first commission), the first generation of the new adult world (Millennium), will certainly not pass away until all these things, including the final commission, have been completed. This task of 'preparing the way' must be done BEFORE King Messiah's return." See "Additional insights" below.

Note this verse: Such is the generation of those who seek him, who seek your face, O God of Jacob. Selah (Palms 24:6)

Additional Insights:

When he returns: Verse 46
Notice what we must be doing when he returns:

Original (Implicit): "It will be good for that servant whose master finds him doing so when he returns."

Paraphrase (Explicit): "This (verse 45 commission) is what I expect you, my disciples, to be doing when I return. (Notice the clear distinction between 'the end' and 'the return'. 'The end' happens in v. 14, many years BEFORE 'the return' which happens after v. 45. The RETURN of Messiah is NOT referred to as 'the end', contrary to virtually all Christian prophecy."

Reward: Verse 47

Original (Implicit): "Truly I tell you, he will put him in charge of all his possessions."

Paraphrase (Explicit): "Truly I tell you, as my disciples, you are joint heirs who will rule and reign with me."

Summary:

In Matthew 24, Jesus is declaring that his followers would initiate two prophetic commissions around a lengthy interval event. The first ends the world as we know it (the childhood world), and begins the kingdom Millennium (the adult world); the second, after the interval, finalizes the place of three people groups – RULERS, CITIZENS, and REBELS, in preparation for Messiah's return. These commissions are the 'two peaks' in his end-of-the-age framework.

This framework is not arbitrary. It is, in fact, a familiar song; the pattern of all spiritual journeys— the Exodus, the Wilderness, and possession of the 'Promised Land'. In type, it is a journey made by Israel, Christianity, and millions of faithful individuals. And now, the Kingdom!

In Mathew 24, we have discovered the Millennium commissions, the central events that 'prepare the way' for the return of the Messiah and his coronation as king. Messiah comes TO a kingdom not to BUILD a kingdom.

How beautiful! Are we prepared to execute these commands?

Did you discover the commissions?

Yes ____   No ____   Maybe ____   How many _____

Comments?

_____

_____

_____

_____

The End-of-the-Age by the Numbers

Being able to summarize a concept is a very strong indicator of truth. Also, it is much easier to assimilate complex subject matter when it is itemized and summarized.

This appendix attempts to do that. It consists largely of summary lists of various aspects of the end-of-the-age and the prophetic model. Prophecy concepts in a nutshell.

The lists can be used as a companion to the longer narrative sections to help organize and reveal the underlying design. They can also be helpful when comparing this prophetic model to others.

An Index of the Lists:

- List 1: Prophecy in a Nutshell
- List 2: Essential Attributes of the End-of-the-Age Prophecy Model
- List 3: Three New Discoveries
- List 4: The Two End-of-the-Age Commissions of Jesus
- List 5: The Three Foundation Scriptures
- List 6: Answering the Three Big End-of-the-Age Questions:
- List 7: The Three Phases of the End-of-the-Age Journey Framework
- List 8: Harvest - Identifying and Perfecting Three People Group
- List 9: The seven 'building block' concepts of prophecy
- List 10: Asking the Priority Questions

List 1: Prophecy in a Nutshell

The Script: The Gospel-of-the-Kingdom

"Comfort, comfort my people, says your God. <u>Speak tenderly to Jerusalem</u>, and proclaim to her that her hard service has been completed, that her sin has been paid for, that she has received from the Lord's hand double for all her sins. A voice of one calling: "In the desert prepare the way for the Lord; make straight in the wilderness a highway for our God. Every valley shall be raised up, every mountain and hill made low; the rough ground shall become level, the rugged places a plain. And the glory of the Lord will be revealed, and all mankind together will see it. For the mouth of the Lord has spoken." (Isaiah 40:1-5)

Our Adult Commission: The Gospel-of-the-Kingdom

And this <u>gospel of the kingdom </u>will be preached in the whole world as a testimony to all nations, and then <u>the end</u> will come. (Matthew 24:14)

Our Adult Destination: All-Truth

"But when he, the Spirit of truth, comes, he will guide you into <u>all truth</u>. He will not speak on his own; he will speak only what he hears, and he will tell you what is yet to come." (John 16:13)

Our Adult Responsibility: Creation

I consider that our present sufferings are not worth comparing with the glory that will be revealed in us. <u>The creation waits in eager expectation for the sons of God to be revealed</u>. For the creation was subjected to frustration, not by its own choice, but by the will of the one who subjected it, in hope that the creation itself will be liberated from its bondage to decay and brought into the glorious freedom of the children of God. (Romans 8:18-21)

List 2: Essential Attributes of the End-of-the-Age Prophecy Model

Resolving a true and systematic prophecy story or model, has been a great challenge to earnest seekers of truth. Today, there are many claims, but sadly, there are no adequate popular models.

We need to ask, "What would constitute a valid prophecy model"? How might we judge any given prophecy model as true (perhaps yours). By design, we believe the end-of-the-age is so unique and complex that it is self-correcting and self-proving.

Below we list our four requirements for a valid prophetic model of the end-of-the-age. **A Prophetic Model must...**

1) **Be Systematic**: Does it include all Biblically prophetic pieces? Do they beautifully fit together as a whole?

2) **Have a Harvest/Adult emphasis:** Does the model emphasize the maturing of mankind's final identities--perfect, good, and evil people groups? (Rather than evangelism, survival, or judgement)

3) **Have a Torah-Centric Framework:** A framework taken from patterns in the Old Testament, not Revelation. The first principle of prophecy is that the 'end' is written in the 'beginning' (Isaiah 46:9,10).

4) **Have a framework clearly illustrated in Jesus' and Paul's prophetic writings:** (see List 5: The Three Foundation Scriptures)

List 3: Three New Discoveries

Assuming this premise, that God wrote the end in the beginning (Torah), and with further study, we will discover three supplemental truths:

1) We will discover the New Testament DOES point to a prophetic framework coming out of Torah.

2) We will find that the Millennium actually begins a generation BEFORE Yeshua returns.

3) We will be confronted with a new and profound ROLE and RESPONSIBILITY for the Body of Messiah.

List 4: The Two End-of-the-Age Commissions of Jesus

When Jesus charged his followers to 'seek first the kingdom...', he was identifying the (only) pathway to a new and glorious world. He was saying the solution to the world's needs and problems is found in the prophetic kingdom.

Based on the New Testament, Jesus delivered only one comprehensive prophecy message that contains a panorama of prophetic end-of-the-age events. Scholars have named this message the 'Olivet Discourse' and the most complete record of it is found in Matthew 24-25 (also Mark 13 & Luke 21).

When we read that message carefully from an adult (what is my role in this) perspective, we find Jesus assigns his followers with two prophetic commissions. These two campaigns, coming from two verses (Matthew 24:14 & 45), point back to two Torah events. Taken together, they use the journey from Egypt to the Promised Land as a framework for the future. This shouldn't surprise us. Israel's journey is everyone's journey ("Out of Egypt I called my son.", Matthew 2:15), including the FRAMEWORK for the end-of-the-age and the kingdom.

This framework, not the current (framework-less) Revelation-centric prophecy, must form the basis for a new prophetic reformation. Paul effectively sees the same framework as Jesus and uses it as the pinnacle of his Romans epistle (Romans 8). There he frames his prophecy with the same two events as Jesus, but thankfully for us, expresses them in different terms. This gives us a 'creation scale' perspective on Jesus' commissions, and our identity.

1) **Commission 1—Exodus**: Jesus: (Matthew 24:14) 'the end'; Paul (Romans 8:19) 'revealing of the sons of God'

2) **Commission 2—Joseph**: Jesus: (Matthew 24:45) 'the greater works'; Paul (Romans 8:29) 'conformed to the likeness of the son' (v29).

List 5: The Three Foundation Scriptures

Here are the three Scriptures which must form the basis of a new prophetic reformation and a valid prophetic model:

1)   **Romans 8:19**: The creation waits in eager expectation for the sons of God to be revealed.

2)   **Matthew 24:14**: And this gospel of the kingdom will be preached in the whole world as a testimony to all nations, and then the end will come.

3)   **Matthew 24:45**: Who then is the faithful and wise servant, whom the master has put in charge of the servants in his household to give them their food at the proper time

List 6: Answering the Three Big End-of-the-Age Questions:

1)   **What is it?**   It is a Restoration—restoring man's original responsibility to manage creation given in the Garden.

2)   **Why must it happen?**   To Harvest the three human people groups (species)—perfecting universal rulers, citizens, and rebels.

3)   **How will it happen?**   With a Journey—patterned after the Biblical account of the Exodus, wilderness, and entry into the Promised Land.

List 7: The Three Phases of the End-of-the-Age Journey Framework

1)   Exodus (Matthew 24:14, Romans 8:19)
2)   Wilderness (Matthew 24:34)
3)   Entering the Promised Land (Matthew 24:45, Romans 8:29)

List 8: Harvest - Identifying and Perfecting Three People Groups

Introduced in the first two chapters of Genesis are three universal concepts—good (holy and common) and evil. The entire human story, the Biblical story, is concerned with cultivating a metaphorical 'crop' of humans. The end-of-the-age is designed to mature, perfect, and harvest the full range of human potential. That human potential is exemplified by the three Genesis concepts. See Chapter 10: Missing the Obvious - Three People Groups. The universal kingdom of God will finally contain:

1) Eternal rulers
2) Eternal citizens
3) Eternal rebels

Does not the potter have the right to make out of the same lump of clay some pottery for noble purposes and some for common use? What if God, choosing to show his wrath and make his power known, bore with great patience the objects of his wrath--prepared for destruction? (Rom 9:21,22)

List 9: The seven 'building block' concepts of prophecy

1)   **Childhood**: The 'hard service', decreed in the Genesis fall of mankind, should be seen as a 'week' of childhood. Human history is framed as a prophetic week of 'labor' with the intent of bringing mankind to adulthood (rest).

2)   **Sabbath**: There yet remains a Sabbath rest. Six and one is (still) a fundamental principle for life and prophecy. The end-of-the-age is structured around the Sabbath principle in various forms. The prophetic week, including Sabbath, is the chronological framework for human history.

3) **Messiah**: Messiah's work was to call 'the adoption' (humans into the divine family). As a group, these have enjoyed childhood for 'two days' (2000 years), but on the 'third day' (start of the Millennium), they will be 'revealed' (as adult), which includes performing 'greater works' prepared from the foundation of the world (see 'Restoration' below), and be conformed to the likeness of Messiah.

4) **Restoration**: Christianity has a prophetic mandate to restore order to human society and government, literally. This new start could be seen as a 'second creation'. This is the ministry the NT refers to as 'preparing the way' and, 'the restitution of all things', performed by a prophetic leader (*'Elijah'*). This restoration is required BEFORE the return of Messiah as king.

5) **Identities**: In God's sovereign design for the human race, he has concealed within it three natures. The fruit of man's 'one-week' labor is a harvest of these three eternal identities, stated in universal terms, as rulers, citizens, and rebels.

6) **Kingdom**: Our adult 'work' begins with the end-of-the-age assignment given to us directly by Jesus—preaching/performing the gospel-of-the-kingdom. It is the world's final testimony of truth and power unlike anything the world has ever seen. However, we cannot fulfil this commission without a structural transformation. See Chapter 4: A NEW PROPHETIC ORDER

7) **Responsibility**: Judgement (responsibility) begins at the house of the Lord—physician heal thyself. To fulfil its mandate to preach the gospel-of-the-kingdom, Jesus' Body must restore its interdependent authority structure (apostle and prophet), with its corresponding separation-of-powers. See Chapter 4: A NEW PROPHETIC ORDER

List 10: Asking Priority Questions

1) How does the kingdom of God actually come to earth? (How will human governance implement and comply with 'God's will on earth as it is in heaven')

2) What is the gospel-of-the-kingdom (Mathew 24:14)?

3) What does 'preparing the way' mean (Isaiah 40:3)?

4) What is 'the restitution of all things' (Acts 3:21)?

5) What is the 'revealing of the sons' (Romans 8:19)?

6) What is 'the end' in Matthew 24:14?

7) What is 'the falling away' in 2 Thessalonians 2:3?